The Complete Works of Oliver Goldsmith

By
Oliver Goldsmith

Anodos
Books

Oliver Wakefield (1728-1766), Henry Austin Dobson (1840-1921).

Originally published in 1906.
Copyright © 2021 Anodos Books. All rights reserved.

Anodos Books
1c Kings Road
Whithorn
Newton Stewart
Dumfries & Galloway
DG8 8PP

Contents

PREFATORY NOTE	1
INTRODUCTION	3
CHRONOLOGY OF GOLDSMITH'S LIFE AND POEMS.	17
DESCRIPTIVE POEMS	21
THE TRAVELLER OR A PROSPECT OF SOCIETY	21
THE DESERTED VILLAGE	32
LYRICAL AND MISCELLANEOUS PIECES	43
PROLOGUE OF LABERIUS	43
ON A BEAUTIFUL YOUTH STRUCK BLIND WITH LIGHTNING	43
THE GIFT TO IRIS, IN BOW STREET	44
THE LOGICIANS REFUTED	44
A SONNET	46
STANZAS ON THE TAKING OF QUEBEC	46
AN ELEGY ON THAT GLORY OF HER SEX, MRS. MARY BLAIZE	46
DESCRIPTION OF AN AUTHOR'S BEDCHAMBER	47
ON SEEING MRS. ** PERFORM IN THE CHARACTER OF ****	48
OF THE DEATH OF THE LEFT HON. ***	48
AN EPIGRAM ADDRESSED TO THE GENTLEMEN REFLECTED ON IN THE ROSCIAD, A POEM, BY THE AUTHOR	49
TO G. C. AND R. L.	49
TRANSLATION OF A SOUTH AMERICAN ODE	49
THE DOUBLE TRANSFORMATION A TALE	49
A NEW SIMILE IN THE MANNER OF SWIFT	52
EDWIN AND ANGELINA A BALLAD	53
ELEGY ON THE DEATH OF A MAD DOG	57
SONG FROM 'THE VICAR OF WAKEFIELD'	58
EPILOGUE TO 'THE GOOD NATUR'D MAN'	59
EPILOGUE TO 'THE SISTER'	59
PROLOGUE TO 'ZOBEIDE'	60

THRENODIA AUGUSTALIS	62
SONG FROM 'SHE STOOPS TO CONQUER'	68
EPILOGUE TO 'SHE STOOPS TO CONQUER'	69
RETALIATION A POEM	70
SONG INTENDED TO HAVE BEEN SUNG IN 'SHE STOOPS TO CONQUER'	74
TRANSLATION ('CHASTE ARE THEIR INSTINCTS')	75
THE HAUNCH OF VENISON A POETICAL EPISTLE TO LORD CLARE	75
EPITAPH ON THOMAS PARNELL	78
THE CLOWN'S REPLY	78
EPITAPH ON EDWARD PURDON	78
EPILOGUE FOR MR. LEE LEWES	78
EPILOGUE INTENDED TO HAVE BEEN SPOKEN FOR 'SHE STOOPS TO CONQUER' (1)	80
EPILOGUE INTENDED TO HAVE BEEN SPOKEN FOR 'SHE STOOPS TO CONQUER' (2)	82
THE CAPTIVITY: AN ORATORIO	83
THE CAPTIVITY	84
VERSES IN REPLY TO AN INVITATION TO DINNER AT DR. BAKER'S.	93
LETTER IN PROSE AND VERSE TO MRS. BUNBURY	94
VIDA'S GAME OF CHESS TRANSLATED	97
NOTES	113

PREFATORY NOTE

This volume is a reprint, extended and revised, of the *Selected Poems* of Goldsmith issued by the Clarendon Press in 1887. It is 'extended,' because it now contains the whole of Goldsmith's poetry: it is 'revised' because, besides the supplementary text, a good deal has been added in the way of annotation and illustration. In other words, the book has been substantially enlarged. Of the new editorial material, the bulk has been collected at odd times during the last twenty years; but fresh Goldsmith facts are growing rare. I hope I have acknowledged obligation wherever it has been incurred; I trust also, for the sake of those who come after me, that something of my own will be found to have been contributed to the literature of the subject.

AUSTIN DOBSON.

Ealing, *September*, 1906.

INTRODUCTION

Two of the earlier, and, in some respects, more important *Memoirs* of Oliver Goldsmith open with a quotation from one of his minor works, in which he refers to the generally uneventful life of the scholar. His own chequered career was a notable exception to this rule. He was born on the 10th of November, 1728, at Pallas,[i] a village in the county of Longford in Ireland, his father, the Rev. Charles Goldsmith, being a clergyman of the Established Church. Oliver was the fifth of a family of five sons and three daughters. In 1730, his father, who had been assisting the rector of the neighbouring parish of Kilkenny West, succeeded to that living, and moved to Lissoy, a hamlet in Westmeath, lying a little to the right of the road from Ballymahon to Athlone. Educated first by a humble relative named Elizabeth Delap, the boy passed subsequently to the care of Thomas Byrne, the village schoolmaster, an old soldier who had fought Queen Anne's battles in Spain, and had retained from those experiences a wandering and unsettled spirit, which he is thought to have communicated to one at least of his pupils. After an attack of confluent small-pox, which scarred him for life, Oliver was transferred from the care of this not-uncongenial preceptor to a school at Elphin. From Elphin he passed to Athlone; from Athlone to Edgeworthstown, where he remained until he was thirteen or fourteen years of age. The accounts of these early days are contradictory. By his schoolfellows he seems to have been regarded as stupid and heavy,—'little better than a fool'; but they admitted that he was remarkably active and athletic, and that he was an adept in all boyish sports. At home, notwithstanding a variable disposition, and occasional fits of depression, he showed to greater advantage. He scribbled verses early; and sometimes startled those about him by unexpected 'swallow-flights' of repartee. One of these, an oft-quoted retort to a musical friend who had likened his awkward antics in a hornpipe to the dancing of Aesop,—

> Heralds! proclaim aloud! all saying,
> See *Aesop* dancing, and his *monkey* playing,—

reads more like a happily-adapted recollection than the actual impromptu of a boy of nine. But another, in which, after a painful silence, he replied to the brutal enquiry of a ne'er-do-well relative as to when he meant to grow handsome, by saying that he would do so when the speaker grew good,—is characteristic of the easily-wounded spirit and 'exquisite sensibility of contempt' with which he was to enter upon the battle of life.

In June, 1744, after anticipating in his own person, the plot of his later play of *She Stoops to Conquer* by mistaking the house of a gentleman at Ardagh for an inn, he was sent to Trinity College, Dublin. The special dress and semi-menial footing of a sizar or poor scholar—for his father, impoverished by the imprudent portioning of his eldest daughter, could not afford to make him a pensioner—were scarcely calculated to modify his personal peculiarities. Added to these, his tutor elect, Dr. Theaker Wilder, was a violent and vindictive man, with whom his ungainly and unhopeful pupil found little favour. Wilder had a passion for mathematics which was not shared by Goldsmith, who, indeed, spoke contemptuously enough of that science in after life. He could, however, he told Malone, 'turn an Ode of Horace into English better than any of them.' But his academic career was not a success.[ii]

In May, 1747, the year in which his father died,—an event that further contracted his already slender means,—he became involved in a college riot, and was publicly admonished. From this disgrace he recovered to some extent in the following month by obtaining a trifling money exhibition, a triumph which he unluckily celebrated by a party at his rooms. Into these festivities, the heinousness of which was aggravated by the fact that they included guests of both sexes, the exasperated Wilder made irruption, and summarily terminated the proceedings by knocking down the host. The disgrace was too much for the poor lad. He forthwith sold his books and belongings, and ran away, vaguely bound for America. But after considerable privations, including the achievement of a destitution so complete that a handful of grey peas, given him by a girl at a wake, seemed a banquet, he turned his steps homeward, and, a reconciliation having been patched up with his tutor, he was received once more at college. In February, 1749, he took his degree, a low one, as B.A., and quitted the university, leaving behind him, for relics of that time, a scratched signature upon a window-pane,[iii] a *folio* Scapula scored liberally with 'promises to pay,' and a reputation for much loitering at the college gates in the study of passing humanity. Another habit which his associates recalled was his writing of ballads when in want of funds. These he would sell at five shillings apiece; and would afterwards steal out in the twilight to hear them sung to the indiscriminate but applauding audience of the Dublin streets.

What was to be done with a genius so unstable, so erratic? Nothing, apparently, but to let him qualify for orders, and for this he is too young. Thereupon ensues a sort of 'Martin's summer' in his changing life,—a disengaged, delightful time when 'Master Noll' wanders irresponsibly from house to house, fishing and flute-playing, or, of winter evenings, taking the chair at the village inn. When at last the moment came for his presentation to the Bishop of Elphin, that prelate, sad to say, rejected him, perhaps because of his college reputation, perhaps because of actual incompetence, perhaps even, as tradition affirms, because he had the bad taste to appear before his examiner in flaming scarlet breeches. After this rebuff, tutoring was next tried. But he had no sooner saved some thirty pounds by teaching, than he threw up his engagement, bought a horse, and started once more for America, by way of Cork. In six weeks he had returned penniless, having substituted for his roadster a sorry jade, to which he gave the contemptuous name of Fiddleback. He had also the simplicity to wonder, on this occasion, that his mother was not rejoiced to see him again. His next ambition was to be a lawyer; and, to this end, a kindly Uncle Contarine equipped him with fifty pounds for preliminary studies. But on his way to London he was decoyed into gambling, lost every farthing, and came home once more in bitter self-abasement. Having now essayed both divinity and law, his next attempt was physic; and, in 1752, fitted out afresh by his long-suffering uncle, he started for, and succeeded in reaching, Edinburgh. Here more memories survive of his social qualities than of his studies; and two years later he left the Scottish capital for Leyden, rather, it may be conjectured, from a restless desire to see the world than really to exchange the lectures of Monro for the lectures of Albinus. At Newcastle (according to his own account) he had the good fortune to be locked up as a Jacobite, and thus escaped drowning, as the ship by which he was to have sailed to Bordeaux sank at the mouth of the Garonne. Shortly afterwards he arrived in Leyden. Gaubius and other Dutch professors figure sonorously in his future works; but whether he had much experimental knowledge of their instructions may be doubted. What seems undeniable is, that the old seduction of play stripped him of every shilling; so that, like Holberg before him, he set out deliberately to make the tour of Europe on foot. *Haud inexpertus loquor,* he wrote in after days, when praising this mode of locomotion. He first visited Flanders. Thence he passed to France, Germany, Switzerland, and Italy, supporting himself mainly by his flute, and by occasional disputations at convents or universities. 'Sir,' said Boswell to Johnson, 'he *disputed* his passage through Europe.' When on the 1st February, 1756, he landed at Dover, it was with empty pockets. But he had sent home to his brother in Ireland his first rough sketch for the poem of *The Traveller*.

He was now seven-and-twenty. He had seen and suffered much, but he was to have further trials before drifting definitely into literature. Between Dover and London, it has been surmised, he made a tentative appearance as a strolling player. His next ascertained part was that of an apothecary's assistant on Fish Street Hill. From this, with the opportune aid of an Edinburgh friend, he proceeded—to use an eighteenth-century phrase—a poor physician[iv] in the Bankside, Southwark, where least of all, perhaps, was London's fabled pavement to be found. So little of it, in fact, fell to Goldsmith's share, that we speedily find him reduced to the rank of reader and corrector of the press to Samuel Richardson, printer, of Salisbury Court, author of *Clarissa*. Later still he is acting as help or substitute in Dr. Milner's 'classical academy' at Peckham. Here, at last, chance seemed to open to him the prospect of a literary life. He had already, says report, submitted a manuscript tragedy to Richardson's judgement; and something he said at Dr. Milner's table attracted the attention of an occasional visitor there, the bookseller Griffiths, who was also proprietor of the *Monthly Review*. He invited Dr. Milner's usher to try his hand at criticism; and finally, in April, 1757, Goldsmith was bound over for a year to that venerable lady whom George Primrose dubs 'the *antiqua mater* of Grub Street'—in other words, he was engaged for bed, board, and a fixed salary to supply copy-of-all-work to his master's magazine.

The arrangement thus concluded was not calculated to endure. After some five months of labour from nine till two, and often later, it came suddenly to an end. No clear explanation of the breach is forthcoming, but mere incompatability of temper would probably supply a sufficient ground for disagreement. Goldsmith, it is said, complained that the bookseller and his wife treated him ill, and denied him ordinary comforts; added to which the lady, a harder taskmistress even than the *antiqua mater* above referred to, joined with her husband in 'editing' his articles, a course which, hard though it may seem, is not unprecedented. However this may be, either in September or October, 1757, he was again upon the world, existing precariously from hand to mouth. 'By a very little practice as a physician, and very little reputation as a poet [a title which, as Prior suggests, possibly means no more than author], I make a shift to live.' So he wrote to his brother-in-law in December. What his literary occupations were cannot be definitely stated; but, if not prepared before, they probably included the translation of a remarkable work issued by Griffiths and others in the ensuing February. This was the *Memoirs of a Protestant, condemned to the Galleys of France for his Religion,* being the authentic record of the sufferings of one Jean Marteilhe of Bergerac, a book of which Michelet has said that it is 'written as if between earth and heaven.' Marteilhe, who died at Cuylenberg in 1777, was living in Holland in 1758; and it may be that Goldsmith had seen or heard of him during his own stay in that country. The translation, however, did not bear Goldsmith's name, but that of James Willington, one of his old class-fellows at Trinity College. Nevertheless, Prior says distinctly that Griffiths (who should have known) declared it to be by Goldsmith.[v] Moreover, the French original had been catalogued in Griffiths' magazine in the second month of Goldsmith's servitude, a circumstance which colourably supplies the reason for its subsequent rendering into English.

The publication of Marteilhe's *Memoirs* had no influence upon Goldsmith's fortunes, for, in a short time, he was again installed at Peckham, in place of Dr. Milner invalided, waiting hopefully for the fulfilment of a promise by his old master to procure him a medical appointment on a foreign station. It is probably that, with a view to provide the needful funds for this expatriation, he now began to sketch the little volume afterwards published under the title of *An Enquiry into the Present State of Polite Learning in Europe*, for towards the middle of the year we find him addressing long letters to his relatives in Ireland to enlist their aid in soliciting subscriptions for this book. At length the desired advancement was obtained,—a nomination as a physician and surgeon to one of the factories on the coast of Coromandel. But banishment to the East Indies was not to be his destiny. For some unexplained reason the project came to nothing; and then—like Roderick Random—he presented himself at Surgeons' Hall for the more modest office of a hospital mate. This was on the 21st of December, 1758. The curt official record states that he was 'found not qualified.' What made matters worse, the necessity for a decent appearance before the examiners had involved him in new obligations to Griffiths, out of which arose fresh difficulties. To pay his landlady, whose husband was arrested for debt, he pawned the suit he had procured by Griffiths' aid; and he also raised money on some volumes which had been sent him for review. Thereupon ensued an angry and humiliating correspondence with the bookseller, as a result of which Griffiths, nevertheless, appears to have held his hand.

By this time Goldsmith had moved into those historic but now non-existent lodgings in 12 Green Arbour Court,[vi] Old Bailey, which have been photographed for ever in Irving's *Tales of a Traveller*. It was here that the foregoing incidents took place; and it was here also that, early in 1759, 'in a wretched dirty room, in which there was but one chair,' the Rev. Thomas Percy, afterwards Bishop of Dromore, found him composing (or more probably correcting the proofs of) *The Enquiry*. 'At least spare invective 'till my book with Mr. Dodsley shall be publish'd,'—he had written not long before to the irate Griffiths—'and then perhaps you may see the bright side of a mind when my professions shall not appear the dictates of necessity but of choice.' *The Enquiry* came out on the 2nd of April. It had no author's name, but it was an open secret that Goldsmith had written it; and to this day it remains to the critic one of the most interesting of his works. Obviously, in a duodecimo of some two hundred widely-printed pages, it was impossible to keep the high-sounding promise of its title; and at best its author's knowledge of the subject, notwithstanding his continental wanderings, can have been but that of an external spectator. Still in an age when critical utterance was more than ordinarily full-wigged and ponderous, it dared to be sprightly and epigrammatic. Some of its passages, besides, bear upon the writer's personal experiences, and serve to piece the imperfections of his biography. If it brought him no sudden wealth, it certainly raised his reputation with the book-selling world. A connexion already begun with Smollett's *Critical Review* was drawn closer; and the shrewd Sosii of the Row began to see the importance of securing so vivacious and unconventional a pen. Towards the end of the year he was writing for Wilkie the collection of periodical essays entitled *The Bee*; and contributing to the same publisher's *Lady's Magazine*, as well as to *The Busy Body* of one Pottinger. In these, more than ever, he was finding his distinctive touch; and ratifying anew, with every fresh stroke of his pen, his bondage to authorship as a calling.

He had still, however, to conquer the public. *The Bee*, although it contains one of his most characteristic essays ('A City Night-Piece'), and some of the most popular of his lighter verses ('The Elegy on Mrs. Mary Blaize'), never attained the circulation essential to healthy existence. It closed with its eighth number in November, 1759. In the following month two gentlemen called at Green Arbour Court to enlist the services of its author. One was Smollett, with a new serial, *The British Magazine*; the other was Johnson's 'Jack Whirler,' bustling Mr. John Newbery from the 'Bible and Sun' in St. Paul's Churchyard, with a new daily newspaper, *The Public Ledger*. For Smollett, Goldsmith wrote the 'Reverie at the Boar's Head Tavern' and the 'Adventures of a Strolling Player,' besides a number of minor papers. For Newbery, by a happy recollection of the *Lettres Persanes* of Montesquieu, or some of his imitators,[vii] he struck almost at once into that charming epistolary series, brimful of fine observation, kindly satire, and various fancy, which was ultimately to become the English classic known as *The Citizen of the World*. He continued to produce these letters periodically until the August of the following year, when they were announced for republication in 'two volumes of the usual *Spectator* size.' In this form they appeared in May, 1762.

But long before this date a change for the better had taken place in

Goldsmith's life. Henceforth he was sure of work,—mere journey-work though much of it must have been;—and, had his nature been less improvident, of freedom from absolute want. The humble lodgings in the Old Bailey were discarded for new premises at No. 6 Wine Office Court, Fleet Street; and here, on the 31st of May, 1761, with Percy, came one whose name was often in the future to be associated with Goldsmith's, the great Dictator of London literary society, Samuel Johnson. Boswell, who made Johnson's acquaintance later, has not recorded the humours of that supper; but it marks the beginning of Goldsmith's friendship with the man who of all others (Reynolds excepted) loved him most and understood him best.

During the remainder of 1761 he continued busily to ply his pen. Besides his contributions to *The Ledger* and *The British Magazine*, he edited *The Lady's Magazine*, inserting in it the *Memoirs of Voltaire*, drawn up some time earlier to accompany a translation of the *Henriade* by his crony and compatriot Edward Purdon. Towards the beginning of 1762 he was hard at work on several compilations for Newbery, for whom he wrote or edited a *History of Mecklenburgh*, and a series of monthly volumes of an abridgement of *Plutarch's Lives*. In October of the same year was published the *Life of Richard Nash*, apparently the outcome of special holiday-visits to the then fashionable watering-place of Bath, whence its fantastic old Master of the Ceremonies had only very lately made his final exit. It is a pleasantly gossiping, and not unedifying little book, which still holds a respectable place among its author's minor works. But a recently discovered entry in an old ledger shows that during the latter half of 1762 he must have planned, if he had not, indeed, already in part composed, a far more important effort, *The Vicar of Wakefield*. For on the 28th of October in this year he sold to one Benjamin Collins, printer, of Salisbury, for 21 pounds, a third in a work with that title, further described as '2 vols. 12mo.' How this little circumstance, discovered by Mr. Charles Welsh when preparing his Life of John Newbery, is to be brought into agreement with the time-honoured story, related (with variations) by Boswell and others, to the effect that Johnson negotiated the sale of the manuscript for Goldsmith when the latter was arrested for rent by his incensed landlady—has not yet been satisfactorily suggested. Possibly the solution is a simple one, referable to some of those intricate arrangements favoured by 'the Trade' at a time when not one but half a score publishers' names figured in an imprint. At present, the fact that Collins bought a third share of the book from the author for twenty guineas, and the statement that Johnson transferred the entire manuscript to a bookseller for sixty pounds, seem irreconcilable. That *The Vicar of Wakefield* was nevertheless written, or was being written, in 1762, is demonstrable from internal evidence.[viii]

About Christmas in the same year Goldsmith moved into lodgings at Islington, his landlady being one Mrs. Elizabeth Fleming, a friend of Newbery, to whose generalship this step seems attributable. From the curious accounts printed by Prior and Forster, it is clear that the publisher was Mrs. Fleming's paymaster, punctually deducting his disbursements from the account current between himself and Goldsmith, an arrangement which as plainly indicates the foresight of the one as it implies the improvidence of the other. Of the work which Goldsmith did for the businesslike and not unkindly little man, there is no very definite evidence; but various prefaces, introductions, and the like, belong to this time; and he undoubtedly was the author of the excellent *History of England in a Series of Letters addressed by a Nobleman to his Son*, published anonymously in June, 1764, and long attributed, for the grace of its style, to Lyttelton, Chesterfield, Orrery, and other patrician pens. Meanwhile his range of acquaintance was growing larger. The establishment, at the beginning of 1764, of the famous association known afterwards as the 'Literary Club' brought him into intimate relations with Beauclerk, Reynolds, Langton, Burke, and others. Hogarth, too, is said to have visited him at Islington, and to have painted the portrait of Mrs. Fleming. Later in the same year, incited thereto by the success of Christopher Smart's *Hannah*, he wrote the Oratorio of *The Captivity*, now to be found in most editions of his poems, but never set to music. Then after the slow growth of months, was issued on the 19th December the elaboration of that fragmentary sketch which he had sent years before to his brother Henry from the Continent, the poem entitled *The Traveller; or, A Prospect of Society*.

In the notes appended to *The Traveller* in the present volume, its origin and progress are sufficiently explained. Its success was immediate and enduring. The beauty of the descriptive passages, the subtle simplicity of the language, the sweetness and finish of the versification, found ready admirers,—perhaps all the more because of the contrast they afforded to the rough and strenuous sounds with which Charles Churchill had lately filled the public ear. Johnson, who contributed a few lines at the close, proclaimed *The Traveller* to be the best poem since the death of Pope; and it is certainly not easy to find its equal among the works of contemporary bards. It at once raised Goldsmith from the condition of a clever newspaper essayist, or—as men like Sir John Hawkins would have said—a mere 'bookseller's drudge,' to the foremost rank among the poets of the day. Another result of its success was the revival of some of his earlier work, which, however neglected by the author, had been freely appropriated by the discerning pirate. In June, 1765, Griffin and Newbery published a little volume of *Essays by Mr. Goldsmith*, including some of the best of his contributions to *The Bee, The Busy Body, The Public Ledger*, and *The British Magazine*, besides 'The Double Transformation' and 'The Logicians Refuted,' two pieces of verse in imitation of Prior and Swift, which have not been traced to an earlier source. To the same year belongs the first version of a poem which he himself regarded as his best work, and which still retains something of its former popularity. This was the ballad of *Edwin and Angelina*, otherwise known as *The Hermit*. It originated in certain metrical discussions with Percy, then engaged upon his famous *Reliques of English Poetry*; and in 1765, Goldsmith, who through his friend Nugent (afterwards Lord Clare) had made the acquaintance of the Earl of Northumberland, printed it privately for the amusement of the Countess. In a revised and amended form it was subsequently given to the world in *The Vicar of Wakefield*.

With the exception of an abortive attempt to resume his practice as a medical man,—an attempt which seems to have been frustrated by the preternatural strength of his prescriptions,—the next memorable thing in Goldsmith's life is the publication of *The Vicar of Wakefield* itself. It made its appearance on the 27th of March, 1766. A second edition followed in May, a third in August. Why, having been sold (in part) to a Salisbury printer as far back as October, 1762, it had remained unprinted so long; and why, when published, it was published by Francis Newbery and not by John Newbery, Goldsmith's employer,—are questions at present unsolved. But the charm of this famous novel is as fresh as when it was first issued. Its inimitable types, its happy mingling of Christianity and character, its wholesome benevolence and its practical wisdom, are still unimpaired. We smile at the inconsistencies of the plot; but we are carried onward in spite of them, captivated by the grace, the kindliness, the gentle humour of the story. Yet it is a mistake to suppose that its success was instantaneous. Pirated it was, of course; but, according to expert investigations, the authorized edition brought so little gain to its first proprietors that the fourth issue of 1770 started with a loss.[ix] The fifth, published in April, 1774, was dated 1773; and had apparently been withheld because the previous edition, which consisted of no more than one thousand copies, was not exhausted. Five years elapsed before the sixth edition made its tardy appearance in 1779. These facts show that the writer's contemporaries were not his most eager readers. But he has long since appealed to the wider audience of posterity; and his fame is not confined to his native country, for he has been translated into most European languages. Dr. Primrose and his family are now veritable 'citizens of the world.'

A selection of *Poems for Young Ladies*, in the 'Moral' division of which he included his own *Edwin and Angelina*; two volumes of *Beauties of English Poesy*, disfigured with strange heedlessness, by a couple of the most objectionable pieces of Prior; a translation of a French history of philosophy, and other occasional work, followed the publication of the *Vicar*. But towards the middle of 1766, he was meditating a new experiment in that line in which Farquhar, Steele, Southerne, and others of his countrymen had succeeded before him. A fervent lover of the stage, he detested the vapid and colourless 'genteel' comedy which had gradually gained ground in England; and he determined to follow up *The Clandestine Marriage*, then recently adapted by Colman and Garrick from Hogarth's *Marriage A-la-Mode*, with another effort of the same class, depending exclusively for its interest upon humour and character. Early in 1767 it was completed, and submitted to Garrick for Drury Lane. But Garrick perhaps too politic to traverse the popular taste, temporized; and eventually after many delays and disappointments, *The Good Natur'd Man*, as it was called, was produced at Covent Garden by Colman on the 29th of January, 1768. Its success was only partial; and in deference to the prevailing craze for the 'genteel,' an admirable scene of low humour had to be omitted in the representation. But the piece, notwithstanding, brought the author 400 pounds, to which the sale of the book, with the condemned passages restored, added another 100 pounds. Furthermore, Johnson, whose 'Suspirius' in *The Rambler* was, under the name of 'Croaker,' one of its most prominent personages, pronounced it to be the best comedy since Cibber's *Provok'd Husband*.

During the autumn of 1767, Goldsmith had again been living at Islington. On this occasion he had a room in Canonbury Tower, Queen Elizabeth's old hunting-lodge, and perhaps occupied the very chamber generally used by John Newbery, whose active life was, in this year, to close. When in London he had modest housing in the Temple. But the acquisition of 500 pounds for *The Good Natur'd Man* seemed to warrant a change of residence, and he accordingly expended four-fifths of that sum for the lease of three rooms on the second floor of No. 2 Brick Court, which he straightway proceeded to decorate sumptuously with mirrors, Wilton carpets, moreen curtains, and Pembroke tables. It was an unfortunate step; and he would have done well to remember the *Nil te quaesiveris extra* with which his inflexible monitor, Johnson, had greeted his apologies for the shortcomings of some earlier lodgings. One of its natural results was to involve him in a new sequence of task-work, from which he never afterwards shook himself free. Hence, following hard upon a *Roman History* which he had already engaged to write for Davies of Russell Street, came a more ambitious project for Griffin, *A History of Animated Nature*; and after this again, another *History of England* for Davies. The pay was not inadequate; for the first he was to have 250 guineas, for the second 800 guineas, and for the last 500 pounds. But as employment for the author of a unique novel, an excellent comedy, and a deservedly successful poem, it was surely—in his own words—'to cut blocks with a razor.'

And yet, apart from the anxieties of growing money troubles, his life could not have been wholly unhappy. There are records of pleasant occasional junketings —'shoe-maker's holidays' he called them—in the still countrified suburbs of Hampstead and Edgware; there was the gathering at the Turk's Head, with its literary magnates, for his severer hours; and for his more pliant moments, the genial 'free-and-easy' or shilling whist-club of a less pretentious kind, where the student of mixed character might shine with something of the old supremacy of George Conway's inn at Ballymahon. And there must have been quieter and more chastened resting-places of memory, when, softening towards the home of his youth, with a sadness made more poignant by the death of his brother Henry in May, 1768, he planned and perfected his new poem of *The Deserted Village*.

In December, 1769, the recent appointment of his friend Reynolds as President of the Royal Academy brought him the honorary office of Professor of History to that institution; and to Reynolds *The Deserted Village* was dedicated. It appeared on the 26th of May, 1770, with a success equal, if not superior, to that of *The Traveller*. It ran through five editions in the year of its publication; and has ever since retained its reputation. If, as alleged, contemporary critics ranked it below its predecessor, the reason advanced by Washington Irving, that the poet had become his own rival, is doubtless correct; and there is always a prejudice in favour of the first success. This, however, is not an obstacle which need disturb the reader now; and he will probably decide that in grace and tenderness of description *The Deserted Village* in no wise falls short of *The Traveller*; and that its central idea, and its sympathy with humanity, give it a higher value as a work of art.

After *The Deserted Village* had appeared, Goldsmith made a short trip to Paris, in company with Mrs. and the two Miss Hornecks, the elder of whom, christened by the poet with the pretty pet-name of 'The Jessamy Bride,' is supposed to have inspired him with more than friendly feelings. Upon his return he had to fall again to the old 'book-building' in order to recruit his exhausted finances. Since his last poem he had published a short *Life of Parnell*; and Davies now engaged him on a *Life of Bolingbroke*, and an abridgement of the *Roman History*. Thus, with visits to friends, among others to Lord Clare, for whom he wrote the delightful occasional verses called *The Haunch of Venison*, the months wore on until, in December, 1770, the print-shops began to be full of the well-known mezzotint which Marchi had engraved from his portrait by Sir Joshua.

His chief publications in the next two years were the above-mentioned *History of England*, 1771; *Threnodia Augustalis*, a poetical lament-to-order on the death of the Princess Dowager of Wales, 1772; and the abridgement of the *Roman History*, 1772. But in the former year he had completed a new comedy, *She Stoops to Conquer; or, The Mistakes of a Night*, which, after the usual vexatious negotiations, was brought out by Colman at Covent Garden on Monday, the 15th of March, 1773. The manager seems to have acted Goldsmith's own creation of 'Croaker' with regard to this piece, and even to the last moment predicted its failure. But it was a brilliant success. More skilful in construction than *The Good Natur'd Man*, more various in its contrasts of character, richer and stronger in humour and *vis comica*, *She Stoops to Conquer* has continued to provide an inexhaustible fund of laughter to more than three generations of playgoers, and still bids fair to retain the character generally given to it, of being one of the three most popular comedies upon the English stage. When published, it was gratefully inscribed, in one of those admirable dedications of which its author above all men possessed the secret, to Johnson, who had befriended it from the first. 'I do not mean,' wrote Goldsmith, 'so much to compliment you as myself. It may do me some honour to inform the public, that I have lived many years in intimacy with you. It may serve the interests of mankind also to inform them, that the greatest wit may be found in a character, without impairing the most unaffected piety.'

His gains from *She Stoops to Conquer* were considerable; but by this time his affairs had reached a stage of complication which nothing short of a miracle could disentangle; and there is reason for supposing that his involved circumstances preyed upon his mind. During the few months of life that remained to him he published nothing, being doubtless sufficiently occupied by the undertakings to which he was already committed. The last of his poetical efforts was the poem entitled *Retaliation*, a group of epitaph-epigrams prompted by some similar *jeux d'esprit* directed against himself by Garrick and other friends, and left incomplete at his death. In March, 1774, the combined effects of work and worry, added to a local disorder, brought on a nervous fever, which he unhappily aggravated by the use of a patent medicine called 'James's Powder.'[x] He had often relied upon this before, but in the present instance it was unsuited to his complaint. On Monday, the 4th of April, 1774, he died, in his forty-sixth year, and was buried on the 9th in the burying-ground of the Temple Church. Two years later a monument, with a medallion portrait by Nollekens, and a Latin inscription by Johnson, was erected to him in Westminster Abbey, at the expense of the Literary Club. But although the inscription contains more than one phrase of felicitous discrimination, notably the oft-quoted *affectuum potens, at lenis dominator*, it may be doubted whether the simpler words used by his rugged old friend in a letter to Langton are not a fitter farewell to Oliver Goldsmith,—'Let not his frailties be remembered; he was a very great man.'

In person Goldsmith was short and strongly built. His complexion was rather fair, but he was deeply scarred with small-pox; and—if we may believe his own account—the vicissitudes and privations of his early life had not tended to diminish his initial disadvantages. 'You scarcely can conceive,' he writes to his brother in 1759, 'how much eight years of disappointment, anguish, and study, have worn me down. . . . Imagine to yourself a pale melancholy visage, with two great wrinkles between the eye-brows, with an eye disgustingly severe, and a big wig; and you may have a perfect picture of my present appearance,' i.e. at thirty years of age. 'I can neither laugh nor drink,' he goes on; 'have contracted an hesitating, disagreeable manner of speaking, and a visage that looks ill-nature itself; in short, I have thought myself into a settled melancholy, and an utter disgust of all that life brings with it.' It is obvious that this description is largely coloured by passing depression. 'His features,' says one contemporary, 'were plain, but not repulsive,—certainly not so when lighted up by conversation.' Another witness—the 'Jessamy Bride'—declares that 'his benevolence was unquestionable, and his countenance bore every trace of it.' His true likeness would seem to lie midway between the grotesquely truthful sketch by Bunbury prefixed in 1776 to the *Haunch of Venison*, and the portrait idealized by personal regard, which Reynolds painted in 1770. In this latter he is shown wearing, in place of his customary wig, his own scant brown hair, and, on this occasion, masquerades in a furred robe, and falling collar. But even through the disguise of a studio 'costume,' the finely-perceptive genius of Reynolds has managed to suggest much that is most appealing in his sitter's nature. Past suffering, present endurance, the craving to be understood, the mute deprecation of contempt, are all written legibly in this pathetic picture. It has been frequently copied, often very ineffectively, for so subtle is the art that the slightest deviation hopelessly distorts and vulgarizes what Reynolds has done supremely, once and for ever.

Goldsmith's character presents but few real complexities. What seems most to have impressed his contemporaries is the difference, emphasized by the happily-antithetic epigram of Garrick, between his written style and his conversation; and collaterally, between his eminence as a literary man and his personal insignificance. Much of this is easily intelligible. He had started in life with few temporal or physical advantages, and with a native susceptibility that intensified his defects. Until he became a middle-aged man, he led a life of which we do not even now know all the degradations; and these had left their mark upon his manners. With the publication of *The Traveller*, he became at once the associate of some of the best talent and intellect in England,—of fine gentlemen such as Beauclerk and Langton, of artists such as Reynolds and Garrick, of talkers such as Johnson and Burke. Morbidly self-conscious, nervously anxious to succeed, he was at once forced into a competition for which neither his antecedents nor his qualifications had prepared him. To this, coupled with the old habit of poverty, must be attributed his oft-cited passion for fine clothes, which surely arose less from vanity than from a mistaken attempt to extenuate what he felt to be his most obvious shortcomings. As a talker especially he was ill-fitted to shine. He was easily disconcerted by retort, and often discomfited in argument. To the end of his days he never lost his native brogue; and (as he himself tells us) he had that most fatal of defects to a narrator, a slow and hesitating manner. The perspicuity which makes the charm of his writings deserted him in conversation; and his best things were momentary flashes. But some of these were undoubtedly very happy. His telling Johnson that he would make the little fishes talk like whales; his affirmation of Burke that he wound into a subject like a serpent; and half-a-dozen other well-remembered examples— afford ample proof of this. Something of the uneasy jealousy he is said to have exhibited with regard to certain of his contemporaries may also be connected with the long probation of obscurity during which he had been a spectator of the good fortune of others, to whom he must have known himself superior. His improvidence seems to have been congenital, since it is to be traced 'even from his boyish days.' But though it cannot justly be ascribed to any reaction from want to sufficiency, it can still less be supposed to have been diminished by that change. If he was careless of money, it must also be remembered that he gave much of it away; and fortune lingers little with those whose ears are always open to a plausible tale of distress. Of his sensibility and genuine kindheartedness there is no doubt. And it is well to remember that most of the tales to his disadvantage come, not from his more distinguished companions, but from such admitted detractors as Hawkins and Boswell. It could be no mean individuality that acquired the esteem, and deserved the regret, of Johnson and Reynolds.

In an edition of Goldsmith's poems, any extended examination of his remaining productions would be out of place. Moreover, the bulk of these is considerably reduced when all that may properly be classed as hack-work has been withdrawn. The histories of Greece, of Rome, and of England; the *Animated Nature*; the lives of Nash, Voltaire, Parnell, and Bolingbroke, are merely compilations, only raised to the highest level in that line because they proceeded from a man whose gift of clear and easy exposition lent a charm to everything he touched. With the work which he did for himself, the case is different. Into *The Citizen of the World*, *The Vicar of Wakefield*, and his two comedies, he put all the best of his knowledge of human nature, his keen sympathy with his kind, his fine common-sense and his genial humour. The same qualities, tempered by a certain grace and tenderness, also enter into the best of his poems. Avoiding the epigram of Pope and the austere couplet of Johnson, he yet borrowed something from each, which he combined with a delicacy and an amenity that he had learned from neither. He himself, in all probability, would have rested his fame on his three chief metrical efforts, *The Traveller*, *The Hermit*, and *The Deserted Village*. But, as is often the case, he is remembered even more favourably by some of those delightful familiar verses, unprinted during his lifetime, which he threw off with no other ambition than the desire to amuse his friends. *Retaliation*, *The Haunch of Venison*, the *Letter in Prose and Verse to Mrs. Bunbury*, all afford noteworthy exemplification of that playful touch and wayward fancy which constitute the chief attraction of this species of poetry. In his imitations of Swift and Prior, and his variations upon French suggestions, his personal note is scarcely so apparent; but the two Elegies and some of the minor pieces retain a deserved reputation. His ingenious prologues and epilogues also serve to illustrate the range and versatility of his talent. As a rule, the arrangement in the present edition is chronological; but it has not been thought necessary to depart from the practice which gives a time-honoured precedence to *The Traveller* and *The Deserted Village*. The true sequence of the poems, in their order of publication, is, however, exactly indicated in the table which follows this Introduction.

CHRONOLOGY OF GOLDSMITH'S LIFE AND POEMS.

1728	*November 10.* Born at Pallas, near Ballymahon, in the county of Longford, Ireland.
1730	Family remove to Lissoy, in the county of Westmeath.
1731	Under Elizabeth Delap.
1734	Under Mr. Thomas Byrne of the village school.
1736–44	At school at Elphin (Mr. Griffin's), Athlone (Mr. Campbell's), Edgeworthstown (Mr. Hughes's).
1744	*June 11.* Admitted a sizar of Trinity College, Dublin, '*annum agens* 15.'
1747	Death of his father, the Rev. Charles Goldsmith. *May.* Takes part in a college riot. *June 15.* Obtains a Smythe exhibition. Runs away from college.
1749	*February 27.* Takes his degree as Bachelor of Arts.
1751	Rejected for orders by the Bishop of Elphin. Tutor to Mr. Flinn. Sets out for America (via Cork), but returns. Letter to Mrs. Goldsmith (his mother).
1752	Starts as a law student, but loses his all at play. Goes to Edinburgh to become a medical student.
1753	*January 13.* Admitted a member of the 'Medical Society' of Edinburgh. *May 8.* Letter to his Uncle Contarine. *September 26.* Letter to Robert Bryanton. Letter to his Uncle Contarine.
1754	Goes to Leyden. Letter to his Uncle Contarine.
1755	*February.* Leaves Leyden. Takes degree of Bachelor of Medicine at Louvain (?). Travels on foot in France, Germany, Switzerland, and Italy. Sketches *The Traveller.*
1756	*February 1.* Returns to Dover. Low comedian; usher (?); apothecary's journeyman; poor physician in Bankside, Southwark.
1757	Press corrector to Samuel Richardson, printer and novelist; assistant at Peckham Academy (Dr. Milner's). *April.* Bound over to Griffiths the bookseller. Quarrels with Griffiths. *December 27.* Letter to his brother-in-law, Daniel Hodson.
1758	*February.* Publishes *The Memoirs of a Protestant, condemned to the Galleys of France for his Religion.* Gives up literature and returns to Peckham. *August.* Leaves Peckham. Letters to Edward Mills, Bryanton, Mrs. Jane Lawder. Appointed surgeon and physician to a factory on the Coast of Coromandel. *November (?).* Letter to Hodson. Moves into 12 Green Arbour Court, Old Bailey. Coromandel appointment comes to nothing. *December 21.* Rejected at Surgeons' Hall as 'not qualified' for a hospital mate.
1759	*February (?).* Letter to Henry Goldsmith. *March.* Visited by Percy at 12 Green Arbour Court. *April 2. Enquiry into the Present State of Polite Learning in Europe* published. 'Prologue of Laberius' (*Enquiry*). *October 6. The Bee* commenced. 'On a Beautiful Youth struck blind with

	Lightning' (*Bee*). *October 13.* 'The Gift' (*Bee*). *October 18.* 'The Logicians Refuted' (*Busy Body*). *October 20.* 'A Sonnet' (*Bee*). *October 22.* 'Stanzas on the Taking of Quebec' (*Busy Body*). *October 27.* 'Elegy on Mrs. Mary Blaize' (*Bee*). *November 24. The Bee* closed.
1760	*January 1. The British Magazine* commenced. *January 12. The Public Ledger* commenced. *January 24.* First Chinese Letter published (*Citizen of the World*). *May 2.* 'Description of an Author's Bedchamber' ('Chinese Letter' in *Public Ledger*). *October 21.* 'On seeing Mrs. . . . perform,' etc. ('Chinese Letter' in *Public Ledger*). Editing *Lady's Magazine*. Compiling Prefaces. Moves into 6 Wine Office Court, Fleet Street.
1761	*March 4.* 'On the Death of the Right Hon. . . . ('Chinese Letter' in *Public Ledger*). *April 4–14.* 'An Epigram'; to G. C. and R. L. ('Chinese Letter in *Public Ledger*). *May 13.* 'Translation of a South American Ode.' ('Chinese Letter' in *Public Ledger*) *August 14.* Last Chinese Letter published (*Citizen of the World*). *Memoirs of M. de Voltaire* published in *Lady's Magazine*.
1762	*February 23.* Pamphlet on Cock Lane Ghost published. *February 26. History of Mecklenburgh* published. *May 1. Citizen of the World* published. *May 1 to Nov. 1. Plutarch's Lives*, vol. i to vii, published. At Bath and Tunbridge. *October 14. Life of Richard Nash* published. *October 28.* Sells third share of *Vicar of Wakefield* to B. Collins, printer, Salisbury. At Mrs. Fleming's at Islington.
1763	*March 31.* Agrees with James Dodsley to write a *Chronological History of the Lives of Eminent Persons of Great Britain and Ireland*. (Never done.)
1764	'The Club,' afterwards the Literary Club, founded. Moves into lodgings on the library staircase of the Temple. *June 26. History of England, in a series of Letters from a Nobleman to his Son* published. *October 31.* Oratorio of *The Captivity* sold to James Dodsley. *December 19. The Traveller* published.
1765	*June 4. Essays by Mr. Goldsmith* published. 'The Double Transformation,' 'A New Simile' (*Essays*). *Edwin and Angelina* (*The Hermit*) printed privately for the amusement of the Countess of Northumberland. Resumes practice as a physician.
1766	*March 27. Vicar of Wakefield* published. 'Elegy on a Mad Dog'; 'Olivia's Song' (*Vicar of Wakefield*). *May 31. Vicar of Wakefield*, 2nd edition. *June.* Translation of Formey's *Concise History of Philosophy and Philosophers* published. *August 29. Vicar of Wakefield*, 3rd edition. *December 15. Poems for Young Ladies* published.
1766	*December 28. English Grammar* written.
1767	*April. Beauties of English Poesy* published. *July 19.* Living in Garden Court, Temple. *July 25.* Letter to the *St. James's Chronicle*. *December 22.* Death of John Newbery.

1768	*February 5.* Publishes *The Good Natur'd Man*, a Comedy, produced at Covent Garden, January 29. 'Epilogue to *The Good Natur'd Man*.' Moves to 2 Brick Court, Middle Temple. *May.* Death of Henry Goldsmith. Living at Edgware.
1769	*February 18.* 'Epilogue to Mrs. Lenox's *Sister*.' *February 29.* Agreement for 'a new Natural History of Animals' (*Animated Nature*). *May 18. Roman History* published. *June 13.* Agreement for *History of England*. *December.* Appointed Professor of History to the Royal Academy.
1770	*January.* Letter to Maurice Goldsmith. *April 24–May 26.* Portrait by Reynolds exhibited. *May 26. The Deserted Village* published. *July 13. Life of Thomas Parnell* published. *July.* On the Continent with the Hornecks. Letters to Reynolds. *September 15.* Agreement for abridgement of *Roman History*. *December 1.* Marchi's print from Reynold's portrait published. *December 19. Life of Bolingbroke* published. *Vicar of Wakefield*, 4th edition.
1771	*Haunch of Venison* written. (?) *August 6. History of England* published. *December 11.* 'Prologue to Cradock's *Zobeide*.'
1772	*February 20. Threnodia Augustalis* published. Watson's Engraving of *Resignation* published. *December.* Abridgement of *Roman History* published.
1773	*March 26.* Publishes *She Stoops to Conquer; or, The Mistakes of a Night*, a Comedy, produced at Covent Garden, March 15. 'Song in *She Stoops to Conquer*,' 'Epilogue to *She Stoops to Conquer*.'
1773	*March 24.* Kenrick's libel in the *London Packet*. *March 31.* Letter in the *Daily Advertiser*. *May 8. The Grumbler* produced. Projects a *Dictionary of Arts and Sciences*.
1774	*March 25.* Illness. *April 4.* Death. *April 9.* 'Buried 9th April, Oliver Goldsmith, MB, late of Brick-court, Middle Temple' (Register of Burials, Temple Church). *April 19. Retaliation* published. *April. Vicar of Wakefield*, 5th edition (dated 1773). *June.* Song ('Ah me, when shall I marry me?') published. *June 28.* Letters of Administration granted. *June. An History of the Earth and Animated Nature* published. 'Translation from Addison.' (*History*, etc., 1774.)
1776	*The Haunch of Venison* published. 'Epitaph on Thomas Parnell,' and 'Two Songs from *The Captivity* (*Haunch of Venison*). Monument with medallion by Nollekens erected in the south transept of Westminster Abbey.
1777	*Poems and Plays* published. 'The Clown's Reply,' 'Epitaph on Edward Purdon' (*Poems*, etc., 1777).
1779	*Vicar of Wakefield*, 6th edition.
1780	*Poetical and Dramatic Works*, Evans's edition, published.

	'Epilogue for Lee Lewes' (*Poetical, etc., Works*, 1780).
1801	*Miscellaneous Works*, Percy's edition, published. 'Epilogues (unspoken) to *She Stoops to Conquer*' (*Misc. Works*, 1801).
1820	*Miscellaneous Works*, 'trade' edition, published. An Oratorio' (*The Captivity*). (*Misc. Works*, 1820.)
1837	*Miscellaneous Works*, Prior's edition, published. 'Verses in Reply to an Invitation to Dinner'; 'Letter in Prose and Verse to Mrs. Bunbury' (*Misc. Works*, 1837). Tablet erected in the Temple Church.
1854	*Goldsmith's Works*, Cunningham's edition, published. 'Translation of Vida's *Game of Chess*' (*Works*, 1854, vol. iv).
1864	*January 5*. J. H. Foley's statue placed in front of Dublin University.

DESCRIPTIVE POEMS

THE TRAVELLER
OR
A PROSPECT OF SOCIETY

DEDICATION
TO THE REV. HENRY GOLDSMITH

Dear Sir,
I am sensible that the friendship between us can acquire no new force from the ceremonies of a Dedication; and perhaps it demands an excuse thus to prefix your name to my attempts, which you decline giving with your own. But as a part of this Poem was formerly written to you from Switzerland, the whole can now, with propriety, be only inscribed to you. It will also throw a light upon many parts of it, when the reader understands, that it is addressed to a man, who, despising Fame and Fortune, has retired early to Happiness and Obscurity, with an income of forty pounds a year.

I now perceive, my dear brother, the wisdom of your humble choice. You have entered upon a sacred office, where the harvest is great, and the labourers are but few; while you have left the field of Ambition, where the labourers are many, and the harvest not worth carrying away. But of all kinds of ambition, what from the refinement of the times, from different systems of criticism, and from the divisions of party, that which pursues poetical fame is the wildest.

Poetry makes a principal amusement among unpolished nations; but in a country verging to the extremes of refinement, Painting and Music come in for a share. As these offer the feeble mind a less laborious entertainment, they at first rival Poetry, and at length supplant her; they engross all that favour once shown to her, and though but younger sisters, seize upon the elder's birthright.

Yet, however this art may be neglected by the powerful, it is still in greater danger from the mistaken efforts of the learned to improve it. What criticisms have we not heard of late in favour of blank verse, and Pindaric odes, choruses, anapaests and iambics, alliterative care and happy negligence! Every absurdity has now a champion to defend it; and as he is generally much in the wrong, so he has always much to say; for error is ever talkative.

But there is an enemy to this art still more dangerous, I mean Party. Party entirely distorts the judgment, and destroys the taste. When the mind is once infected with this disease, it can only find pleasure in what contributes to increase the distemper. Like the tiger, that seldom desists from pursuing man after having once preyed upon human flesh, the reader, who has once gratified his appetite with calumny, makes, ever after, the most agreeable feast upon murdered reputation. Such readers generally admire some half-witted thing, who wants to be thought a bold man, having lost the character of a wise one. Him they dignify with the name of poet; his tawdry lampoons are called satires, his turbulence is said to be force, and his frenzy fire.

What reception a Poem may find, which has neither abuse, party, nor blank verse to support it, I cannot tell, nor am I solicitous to know. My aims are right. Without espousing the cause of any party, I have attempted to moderate the rage of all. I have endeavoured to show, that there may be equal happiness in states, that are differently governed from our own; that every state has a particular principle of happiness, and that this principle in each may be carried to a mischievous excess. There are few can judge, better than yourself, how far these positions are illustrated in this Poem.

    I am, dear Sir,
Your most affectionate Brother,
        OLIVER GOLDSMITH.

THE TRAVELLER

OR

A PROSPECT OF SOCIETY

<pre>
REMOTE, unfriended, melancholy, slow,
Or by the lazy Scheldt, or wandering Po;
Or onward, where the rude Carinthian boor
Against the houseless stranger shuts the door;
Or where Campania's plain forsaken lies,   5
A weary waste expanding to the skies:
Where'er I roam, whatever realms to see,
My heart untravell'd fondly turns to thee;
Still to my brother turns with ceaseless pain,
And drags at each remove a lengthening chain.   10

  Eternal blessings crown my earliest friend,
And round his dwelling guardian saints attend:
Bless'd be that spot, where cheerful guests retire
To pause from toil, and trim their ev'ning fire;
Bless'd that abode, where want and pain repair,   15
And every stranger finds a ready chair;
Bless'd be those feasts with simple plenty crown'd,
Where all the ruddy family around
Laugh at the jests or pranks that never fail,
Or sigh with pity at some mournful tale,   20
Or press the bashful stranger to his food,
</pre>

And learn the luxury of doing good.

But me, not destin'd such delights to share,
My prime of life in wand'ring spent and care,
Impell'd, with steps unceasing, to pursue   25
Some fleeting good, that mocks me with the view;
That, like the circle bounding earth and skies,
Allures from far, yet, as I follow, flies;
My fortune leads to traverse realms alone,
And find no spot of all the world my own.   30

E'en now, where Alpine solitudes ascend,
I sit me down a pensive hour to spend;
And, plac'd on high above the storm's career,
Look downward where a hundred realms appear;
Lakes, forests, cities, plains, extending wide,   35
The pomp of kings, the shepherd's humbler pride.

When thus Creation's charms around combine,
Amidst the store, should thankless pride repine?
Say, should the philosophic mind disdain
That good, which makes each humbler bosom vain?   40
Let school-taught pride dissemble all it can,
These little things are great to little man;
And wiser he, whose sympathetic mind
Exults in all the good of all mankind.
Ye glitt'ring towns, with wealth and splendour crown'd,   45
Ye fields, where summer spreads profusion round,
Ye lakes, whose vessels catch the busy gale,
Ye bending swains, that dress the flow'ry vale,
For me your tributary stores combine;
Creation's heir, the world, the world is mine!   50

As some lone miser visiting his store,
Bends at his treasure, counts, re-counts it o'er;
Hoards after hoards his rising raptures fill,
Yet still he sighs, for hoards are wanting still:
Thus to my breast alternate passions rise,   55
Pleas'd with each good that heaven to man supplies:
Yet oft a sigh prevails, and sorrows fall,
To see the hoard of human bliss so small;
And oft I wish, amidst the scene, to find
Some spot to real happiness consign'd,   60
Where my worn soul, each wand'ring hope at rest,
May gather bliss to see my fellows bless'd.

But where to find that happiest spot below,
Who can direct, when all pretend to know?
The shudd'ring tenant of the frigid zone   65

Boldly proclaims that happiest spot his own,
Extols the treasures of his stormy seas,
And his long nights of revelry and ease;
The naked negro, panting at the line,
Boasts of his golden sands and palmy wine,   70
Basks in the glare, or stems the tepid wave,
And thanks his gods for all the good they gave.
Such is the patriot's boast, where'er we roam,
His first, best country ever is, at home.
And yet, perhaps, if countries we compare,   75
And estimate the blessings which they share,
Though patriots flatter, still shall wisdom find
An equal portion dealt to all mankind,
As different good, by Art or Nature given,
To different nations makes their blessings even.   80

  Nature, a mother kind alike to all,
Still grants her bliss at Labour's earnest call;
With food as well the peasant is supplied
On Idra's cliffs as Arno's shelvy side;
And though the rocky-crested summits frown,   85
These rocks, by custom, turn to beds of down.
From Art more various are the blessings sent;
Wealth commerce, honour, liberty, content.
Yet these each other's power so strong contest,
That either seems destructive of the rest.   90
Where wealth and freedom reign, contentment fails,
And honour sinks where commerce long prevails.
Hence every state to one lov'd blessing prone,
Conforms and models life to that alone.
Each to the favourite happiness attends,   95
And spurns the plan that aims at other ends;
Till, carried to excess in each domain,
This favourite good begets peculiar pain.

  But let us try these truths with closer eyes,
And trace them through the prospect as it lies: 100
Here for a while my proper cares resign'd,
Here let me sit in sorrow for mankind,
Like yon neglected shrub at random cast,
That shades the steep, and sighs at every blast.

  Far to the right where Apennine ascends,   105
Bright as the summer, Italy extends;
Its uplands sloping deck the mountain's side,
Woods over woods in gay theatric pride;
While oft some temple's mould'ring tops between
With venerable grandeur mark the scene   110

   Could Nature's bounty satisfy the breast,
The sons of Italy were surely blest.
Whatever fruits in different climes were found,
That proudly rise, or humbly court the ground;
Whatever blooms in torrid tracts appear,   115
Whose bright succession decks the varied year;
Whatever sweets salute the northern sky
With vernal lives that blossom but to die;
These here disporting own the kindred soil,
Nor ask luxuriance from the planter's toil;   120
While sea-born gales their gelid wings expand
To winnow fragrance round the smiling land.

   But small the bliss that sense alone bestows,
And sensual bliss is all the nation knows.
In florid beauty groves and fields appear,   125
Man seems the only growth that dwindles here.
Contrasted faults through all his manner reign;
Though poor, luxurious; though submissive, vain;
Though grave, yet trifling; zealous, yet untrue;
And e'en in penance planning sins anew.   130
All evils here contaminate the mind,
That opulence departed leaves behind;
For wealth was theirs, not far remov'd the date,
When commerce proudly flourish'd through the state;
At her command the palace learn'd to rise,   135
Again the long-fall'n column sought the skies;
The canvas glow'd beyond e'en Nature warm,
The pregnant quarry teem'd with human form;
Till, more unsteady than the southern gale,
Commerce on other shores display'd her sail;   140
While nought remain'd of all that riches gave,
But towns unmann'd, and lords without a slave;
And late the nation found, with fruitless skill,
Its former strength was but plethoric ill.

   Yet still the loss of wealth is here supplied   145
By arts, the splendid wrecks of former pride;
From these the feeble heart and long-fall'n mind
An easy compensation seem to find.
Here may be seen, in bloodless pomp array'd,
The paste-board triumph and the cavalcade;   150
Processions form'd for piety and love,
A mistress or a saint in every grove.
By sports like these are all their cares beguil'd,
The sports of children satisfy the child;
Each nobler aim, repress'd by long control,   155
Now sinks at last, or feebly mans the soul;

While low delights, succeeding fast behind,
In happier meanness occupy the mind:
As in those domes, where Caesars once bore sway,
Defac'd by time and tottering in decay,   160
There in the ruin, heedless of the dead,
The shelter-seeking peasant builds his shed,
And, wond'ring man could want the larger pile,
Exults, and owns his cottage with a smile.

  My soul, turn from them; turn we to survey   165
Where rougher climes a nobler race display,
Where the bleak Swiss their stormy mansions tread,
And force a churlish soil for scanty bread;
No product here the barren hills afford,
But man and steel, the soldier and his sword;   170
No vernal blooms their torpid rocks array,
But winter ling'ring chills the lap of May;
No Zephyr fondly sues the mountain's breast,
But meteors glare, and stormy glooms invest.

  Yet still, e'en here, content can spread a charm,   175
Redress the clime, and all its rage disarm.
Though poor the peasant's hut, his feasts though small,
He sees his little lot the lot of all;
Sees no contiguous palace rear its head
To shame the meanness of his humble shed;   180
No costly lord the sumptuous banquet deal
To make him loathe his vegetable meal;
But calm, and bred in ignorance and toil,
Each wish contracting, fits him to the soil.
Cheerful at morn he wakes from short repose,   185
Breasts the keen air, and carols as he goes;
With patient angle trolls the finny deep,
Or drives his vent'rous plough-share to the steep;
Or seeks the den where snow-tracks mark the way,
And drags the struggling savage into day.   190
At night returning, every labour sped,
He sits him down the monarch of a shed;
Smiles by his cheerful fire, and round surveys
His children's looks, that brighten at the blaze;
While his lov'd partner, boastful of her hoard,   195
Displays her cleanly platter on the board:
And haply too some pilgrim, thither led,
With many a tale repays the nightly bed.

  Thus every good his native wilds impart,
Imprints the patriot passion on his heart,   200
And e'en those ills, that round his mansion rise,

Enhance the bliss his scanty fund supplies.
Dear is that shed to which his soul conforms,
And dear that hill which lifts him to the storms; 205
And as a child, when scaring sounds molest,
Clings close and closer to the mother's breast,
So the loud torrent, and the whirlwind's roar,
But bind him to his native mountains more.

  Such are the charms to barren states assign'd;
Their wants but few, their wishes all confin'd. 210
Yet let them only share the praises due,
If few their wants, their pleasures are but few;
For every want that stimulates the breast,
Becomes a source of pleasure when redrest.
Whence from such lands each pleasing science flies, 215
That first excites desire, and then supplies;
Unknown to them, when sensual pleasures cloy,
To fill the languid pause with finer joy;
Unknown those powers that raise the soul to flame,
Catch every nerve, and vibrate through the frame. 220
Their level life is but a smould'ring fire,
Unquench'd by want, unfann'd by strong desire;
Unfit for raptures, or, if raptures cheer
On some high festival of once a year,
In wild excess the vulgar breast takes fire, 225
Till, buried in debauch, the bliss expire.

  But not their joys alone thus coarsely flow:
Their morals, like their pleasures, are but low;
For, as refinement stops, from sire to son
Unalter'd, unimprov'd the manners run; 230
And love's and friendship's finely pointed dart
Fall blunted from each indurated heart.
Some sterner virtues o'er the mountain's breast
May sit, like falcons cow'ring on the nest;
But all the gentler morals, such as play 235
Through life's more cultur'd walks, and charm the way,
These far dispers'd, on timorous pinions fly,
To sport and flutter in a kinder sky.

  To kinder skies, where gentler manners reign,
I turn; and France displays her bright domain. 240
Gay sprightly land of mirth and social ease,
Pleas'd with thyself, whom all the world can please,
How often have I led thy sportive choir,
With tuneless pipe, beside the murmuring Loire!
Where shading elms along the margin grew, 245
And freshen'd from the wave the Zephyr flew;

And haply, though my harsh touch falt'ring still,
But mock'd all tune, and marr'd the dancer's skill;
Yet would the village praise my wondrous power,
And dance, forgetful of the noon-tide hour.   250
Alike all ages. Dames of ancient days
Have led their children through the mirthful maze,
And the gay grandsire, skill'd in gestic lore,
Has frisk'd beneath the burthen of threescore.

  So bless'd a life these thoughtless realms display,   255
Thus idly busy rolls their world away:
Theirs are those arts that mind to mind endear,
For honour forms the social temper here:
Honour, that praise which real merit gains,
Or e'en imaginary worth obtains,   260
Here passes current; paid from hand to hand,
It shifts in splendid traffic round the land:
From courts, to camps, to cottages it strays,
And all are taught an avarice of praise;
They please, are pleas'd, they give to get esteem,   265
Till, seeming bless'd, they grow to what they seem.

  But while this softer art their bliss supplies,
It gives their follies also room to rise;
For praise too dearly lov'd, or warmly sought,
Enfeebles all internal strength of thought;   270
And the weak soul, within itself unblest,
Leans for all pleasure on another's breast.
Hence ostentation here, with tawdry art,
Pants for the vulgar praise which fools impart;
Here vanity assumes her pert grimace,   275
And trims her robes of frieze with copper lace;
Here beggar pride defrauds her daily cheer,
To boast one splendid banquet once a year;
The mind still turns where shifting fashion draws,
Nor weighs the solid worth of self-applause.   280

  To men of other minds my fancy flies,
Embosom'd in the deep where Holland lies.
Methinks her patient sons before me stand,
Where the broad ocean leans against the land,
And, sedulous to stop the coming tide,   285
Lift the tall rampire's artificial pride.
Onward, methinks, and diligently slow,
The firm-connected bulwark seems to grow;
Spreads its long arms amidst the wat'ry roar,
Scoops out an empire, and usurps the shore;   290
While the pent ocean rising o'er the pile,

Sees an amphibious world beneath him smile;
The slow canal, the yellow-blossom'd vale,
The willow-tufted bank, the gliding sail,
The crowded mart, the cultivated plain,   295
A new creation rescu'd from his reign.

 Thus, while around the wave-subjected soil
Impels the native to repeated toil,
Industrious habits in each bosom reign,
And industry begets a love of gain.   300
Hence all the good from opulence that springs,
With all those ills superfluous treasure brings,
Are here displayed. Their much-lov'd wealth imparts
Convenience, plenty, elegance, and arts;
But view them closer, craft and fraud appear,   305
E'en liberty itself is barter'd here.
At gold's superior charms all freedom flies,
The needy sell it, and the rich man buys;
A land of tyrants, and a den of slaves,
Here wretches seek dishonourable graves,   310
And calmly bent, to servitude conform,
Dull as their lakes that slumber in the storm.

 Heavens! how unlike their Belgic sires of old!
Rough, poor, content, ungovernably bold;
War in each breast, and freedom on each brow;   315
How much unlike the sons of Britain now!

 Fir'd at the sound, my genius spreads her wing,
And flies where Britain courts the western spring;
Where lawns extend that scorn Arcadian pride,
And brighter streams than fam'd Hydaspes glide.   320
There all around the gentlest breezes stray,
There gentle music melts on ev'ry spray;
Creation's mildest charms are there combin'd,
Extremes are only in the master's mind!
Stern o'er each bosom reason holds her state,   325
With daring aims irregularly great;
Pride in their port, defiance in their eye,
I see the lords of human kind pass by,
Intent on high designs, a thoughtful band,
By forms unfashion'd, fresh from Nature's hand;   330
Fierce in their native hardiness of soul,
True to imagin'd right, above control,
While e'en the peasant boasts these rights to scan,
And learns to venerate himself as man.

 Thine, Freedom, thine the blessings pictur'd here,   335
Thine are those charms that dazzle and endear;

Too bless'd, indeed, were such without alloy,
But foster'd e'en by Freedom, ills annoy:
That independence Britons prize too high,
Keeps man from man, and breaks the social tie;   340
The self-dependent lordlings stand alone,
All claims that bind and sweeten life unknown;
Here by the bonds of nature feebly held,
Minds combat minds, repelling and repell'd.
Ferments arise, imprison'd factions roar,   345
Repress'd ambition struggles round her shore,
Till over-wrought, the general system feels
Its motions stop, or frenzy fire the wheels.

  Nor this the worst. As nature's ties decay,
As duty, love, and honour fail to sway,   350
Fictitious bonds, the bonds of wealth and law,
Still gather strength, and force unwilling awe.
Hence all obedience bows to these alone,
And talent sinks, and merit weeps unknown;
Time may come, when stripp'd of all her charms,   355
The land of scholars, and the nurse of arms,
Where noble stems transmit the patriot flame,
Where kings have toil'd, and poets wrote for fame,
One sink of level avarice shall lie,
And scholars, soldiers, kings, unhonour'd die.   360

  Yet think not, thus when Freedom's ills I state,
I mean to flatter kings, or court the great;
Ye powers of truth, that bid my soul aspire,
Far from my bosom drive the low desire;
And thou, fair Freedom, taught alike to feel   365
The rabble's rage, and tyrant's angry steel;
Thou transitory flower, alike undone
By proud contempt, or favour's fostering sun,
Still may thy blooms the changeful clime endure,
I only would repress them to secure: 370
For just experience tells, in every soil,
That those who think must govern those that toil;
And all that freedom's highest aims can reach,
Is but to lay proportion'd loads on each.
Hence, should one order disproportion'd grow,   375
Its double weight must ruin all below.

  O then how blind to all that truth requires,
Who think it freedom when a part aspires!
Calm is my soul, nor apt to rise in arms,
Except when fast-approaching danger warms: 380
But when contending chiefs blockade the throne,

Contracting regal power to stretch their own;
When I behold a factious band agree
To call it freedom when themselves are free;
Each wanton judge new penal statutes draw, 385
Laws grind the poor, and rich men rule the law;
The wealth of climes, where savage nations roam,
Pillag'd from slaves to purchase slaves at home;
Fear, pity, justice, indignation start,
Tear off reserve, and bare my swelling heart; 390
Till half a patriot, half a coward grown,
I fly from petty tyrants to the throne.

  Yes, brother, curse with me that baleful hour,
When first ambition struck at regal power;
And thus polluting honour in its source, 395
Gave wealth to sway the mind with double force.
Have we not seen, round Britain's peopled shore,
Her useful sons exchang'd for useless ore?
Seen all her triumphs but destruction haste,
Like flaring tapers bright'ning as they waste; 400
Seen opulence, her grandeur to maintain,
Lead stern depopulation in her train,
And over fields where scatter'd hamlets rose,
In barren solitary pomp repose?
Have we not seen, at pleasure's lordly call, 405
The smiling long-frequented village fall?
Beheld the duteous son, the sire decay'd,
The modest matron, and the blushing maid,
Forc'd from their homes, a melancholy train,
To traverse climes beyond the western main; 410
Where wild Oswego spreads her swamps around,
And Niagara stuns with thund'ring sound?

  E'en now, perhaps as there some pilgrim strays
Through tangled forests, and through dangerous ways;
Where beasts with man divided empire claim, 415
And the brown Indian marks with murd'rous aim;
There, while above the giddy tempest flies,
And all around distressful yells arise,
The pensive exile, bending with his woe,
To stop too fearful, and too faint to go, 420
Casts a long look where England's glories shine,
And bids his bosom sympathise with mine.

  Vain, very vain, my weary search to find
That bliss which only centres in the mind:
Why have I stray'd from pleasure and repose, 425
To seek a good each government bestows?

In every government, though terrors reign,
Though tyrant kings, or tyrant laws restrain,
How small, of all that human hearts endure,
That part which laws or kings can cause or cure.   430
Still to ourselves in every place consign'd,
Our own felicity we make or find:
With secret course, which no loud storms annoy,
Glides the smooth current of domestic joy.
The lifted axe, the agonising wheel,   435
Luke's iron crown, and Damiens' bed of steel,
To men remote from power but rarely known,
Leave reason, faith, and conscience all our own.

THE DESERTED VILLAGE

DEDICATION
TO SIR JOSHUA REYNOLDS

Dear Sir,
I can have no expectations in an address of this kind, either to add to your reputation, or to establish my own. You can gain nothing from my admiration, as I am ignorant of that art in which you are said to excel; and I may lose much by the severity of your judgment, as few have a juster taste in poetry than you. Setting interest therefore aside, to which I never paid much attention, I must be indulged at present in following my affections. The only dedication I ever made was to my brother, because I loved him better than most other men. He is since dead. Permit me to inscribe this Poem to you.

How far you may be pleased with the versification and mere mechanical parts of this attempt, I don't pretend to enquire; but I know you will object (and indeed several of our best and wisest friends concur in the opinion) that the depopulation it deplores is no where to be seen, and the disorders it laments are only to be found in the poet's own imagination. To this I can scarce make any other answer than that I sincerely believe what I have written; that I have taken all possible pains, in my country excursions, for these four or five years past, to be certain of what I allege; and that all my views and enquiries have led me to believe those miseries real, which I here attempt to display. But this is not the place to enter into an enquiry, whether the country be depopulating or not; the discussion would take up much room, and I should prove myself, at best, an indifferent politician, to tire the reader with a long preface, when I want his unfatigued attention to a long poem.

In regretting the depopulation of the country, I inveigh against the increase of our luxuries; and here also I expect the shout of modern politicians against me. For twenty or thirty years past, it has been the fashion to consider luxury as one of the greatest national advantages; and all the wisdom of antiquity in that particular, as erroneous. Still however, I must remain a professed ancient on that head, and continue to think those luxuries prejudicial to states, by which so many vices are introduced, and so many kingdoms have been undone. Indeed so much has been poured out of late on the other side of the question, that, merely for the sake of novelty and variety, one would sometimes wish to be in the right.

    I am, Dear Sir,
Your sincere friend, and ardent admirer,
                  OLIVER GOLDSMITH.

THE DESERTED VILLAGE

SWEET AUBURN! loveliest village of the plain,
Where health and plenty cheer'd the labouring swain,
Where smiling spring its earliest visit paid,
And parting summer's lingering blooms delay'd:
Dear lovely bowers of innocence and ease,   5
Seats of my youth, when every sport could please,
How often have I loiter'd o'er thy green,
Where humble happiness endear'd each scene;
How often have I paus'd on every charm,
The shelter'd cot, the cultivated farm,   10
The never-failing brook, the busy mill,
The decent church that topp'd the neighbouring hill,
The hawthorn bush, with seats beneath the shade,
For talking age and whisp'ring lovers made;
How often have I bless'd the coming day,   15
When toil remitting lent its turn to play,
And all the village train, from labour free,
Led up their sports beneath the spreading tree;
While many a pastime circled in the shade,
The young contending as the old survey'd;   20
And many a gambol frolick'd o'er the ground,
And sleights of art and feats of strength went round;
And still as each repeated pleasure tir'd,
Succeeding sports the mirthful band inspir'd;
The dancing pair that simply sought renown,   25
By holding out to tire each other down;
The swain mistrustless of his smutted face,
While secret laughter titter'd round the place;
The bashful virgin's side-long looks of love,
The matron's glance that would those looks reprove: 30
These were thy charms, sweet village; sports like these,
With sweet succession, taught e'en toil to please;

These round thy bowers their cheerful influence shed,
These were thy charms—But all these charms are fled.

   Sweet smiling village, loveliest of the lawn,   35
Thy sports are fled, and all thy charms withdrawn;
Amidst thy bowers the tyrant's hand is seen,
And desolation saddens all thy green:
One only master grasps the whole domain,
And half a tillage stints thy smiling plain: 40
No more thy glassy brook reflects the day,
But chok'd with sedges, works its weedy way.
Along thy glades, a solitary guest,
The hollow-sounding bittern guards its nest;
Amidst thy desert walks the lapwing flies,   45
And tires their echoes with unvaried cries.
Sunk are thy bowers in shapeless ruin all,
And the long grass o'ertops the mould'ring wall;
And trembling, shrinking from the spoiler's hand,
Far, far away, thy children leave the land.   50

   Ill fares the land, to hast'ning ills a prey,
Where wealth accumulates, and men decay:
Princes and lords may flourish, or may fade;
A breath can make them, as a breath has made;
But a bold peasantry, their country's pride,   55
When once destroy'd, can never be supplied.

   A time there was, ere England's griefs began,
When every rood of ground maintain'd its man;
For him light labour spread her wholesome store,
Just gave what life requir'd, but gave no more: 60
His best companions, innocence and health;
And his best riches, ignorance of wealth.

   But times are alter'd; trade's unfeeling train
Usurp the land and dispossess the swain;
Along the lawn, where scatter'd hamlets rose,   65
Unwieldy wealth, and cumbrous pomp repose;
And every want to opulence allied,
And every pang that folly pays to pride.
Those gentle hours that plenty bade to bloom,
Those calm desires that ask'd but little room,   70
Those healthful sports that grac'd the peaceful scene,
Liv'd in each look, and brighten'd all the green;
These, far departing, seek a kinder shore,
And rural mirth and manners are no more.

   Sweet AUBURN! parent of the blissful hour,   75
Thy glades forlorn confess the tyrant's power.

Here as I take my solitary rounds,
Amidst thy tangling walks, and ruin'd grounds,
And, many a year elaps'd, return to view
Where once the cottage stood, the hawthorn grew, 80
Remembrance wakes with all her busy train,
Swells at my breast, and turns the past to pain.

  In all my wand'rings round this world of care,
In all my griefs—and GOD has given my share—
I still had hopes my latest hours to crown, 85
Amidst these humble bowers to lay me down;
To husband out life's taper at the close,
And keep the flame from wasting by repose.
I still had hopes, for pride attends us still,
Amidst the swains to show my book-learn'd skill, 90
Around my fire an evening group to draw,
And tell of all I felt, and all I saw;
And, as a hare, whom hounds and horns pursue,
Pants to the place from whence at first she flew,
I still had hopes, my long vexations pass'd, 95
Here to return—and die at home at last.

  O blest retirement, friend to life's decline,
Retreats from care, that never must be mine,
How happy he who crowns in shades like these,
A youth of labour with an age of ease; 100
Who quits a world where strong temptations try
And, since 'tis hard to combat, learns to fly!
For him no wretches, born to work and weep,
Explore the mine, or tempt the dangerous deep;
No surly porter stands in guilty state 105
To spurn imploring famine from the gate;
But on he moves to meet his latter end,
Angels around befriending Virtue's friend;
Bends to the grave with unperceiv'd decay,
While Resignation gently slopes the way; 110
And, all his prospects bright'ning to the last,
His Heaven commences ere the world be pass'd!

  Sweet was the sound, when oft at evening's close
Up yonder hill the village murmur rose;
There, as I pass'd with careless steps and slow, 115
The mingling notes came soften'd from below;
The swain responsive as the milk-maid sung,
The sober herd that low'd to meet their young;
The noisy geese that gabbled o'er the pool,
The playful children just let loose from school; 120
The watchdog's voice that bay'd the whisp'ring wind,

And the loud laugh that spoke the vacant mind;
These all in sweet confusion sought the shade,
And fill'd each pause the nightingale had made.
But now the sounds of population fail,   125
No cheerful murmurs fluctuate in the gale,
No busy steps the grass-grown foot-way tread,
For all the bloomy flush of life is fled.
All but yon widow'd, solitary thing
That feebly bends beside the plashy spring;   130
She, wretched matron, forc'd in age, for bread,
To strip the brook with mantling cresses spread,
To pick her wintry faggot from the thorn,
To seek her nightly shed, and weep till morn;
She only left of all the harmless train,   135
The sad historian of the pensive plain.

  Near yonder copse, where once the garden smil'd,
And still where many a garden flower grows wild;
There, where a few torn shrubs the place disclose,
The village preacher's modest mansion rose.   140
A man he was to all the country dear,
And passing rich with forty pounds a year;
Remote from towns he ran his godly race,
Nor e'er had chang'd, nor wished to change his place;
Unpractis'd he to fawn, or seek for power,   145
By doctrines fashion'd to the varying hour;
Far other aims his heart had learned to prize,
More skill'd to raise the wretched than to rise.
His house was known to all the vagrant train,
He chid their wand'rings, but reliev'd their pain;   150
The long-remember'd beggar was his guest,
Whose beard descending swept his aged breast;
The ruin'd spendthrift, now no longer proud,
Claim'd kindred there, and had his claims allow'd;
The broken soldier, kindly bade to stay,   155
Sat by his fire, and talk'd the night away;
Wept o'er his wounds, or tales of sorrow done,
Shoulder'd his crutch, and show'd how fields were won.
Pleas'd with his guests, the good man learn'd to glow,
And quite forgot their vices in their woe;   160
Careless their merits, or their faults to scan,
His pity gave ere charity began.

  Thus to relieve the wretched was his pride,
And e'en his failings lean'd to Virtue's side;
But in his duty prompt at every call,   165
He watch'd and wept, he pray'd and felt, for all.
And, as a bird each fond endearment tries

To tempt its new-fledg'd offspring to the skies,
He tried each art, reprov'd each dull delay,
Allur'd to brighter worlds, and led the way.   170

  Beside the bed where parting life was laid,
And sorrow, guilt, and pain, by turns dismay'd,
The reverend champion stood. At his control,
Despair and anguish fled the struggling soul;
Comfort came down the trembling wretch to raise,   175
And his last falt'ring accents whisper'd praise.

  At church, with meek and unaffected grace,
His looks adorn'd the venerable place;
Truth from his lips prevail'd with double sway,
And fools, who came to scoff, remain'd to pray.   180
The service pass'd, around the pious man,
With steady zeal, each honest rustic ran;
Even children follow'd with endearing wile,
And pluck'd his gown, to share the good man's smile.
His ready smile a parent's warmth express'd,   185
Their welfare pleas'd him, and their cares distress'd;
To them his heart, his love, his griefs were given,
But all his serious thoughts had rest in Heaven.
As some tall cliff, that lifts its awful form,
Swells from the vale, and midway leaves the storm,   190
Though round its breast the rolling clouds are spread,
Eternal sunshine settles on its head.

  Beside yon straggling fence that skirts the way,
With blossom'd furze unprofitably gay,
There, in his noisy mansion, skill'd to rule,   195
The village master taught his little school;
A man severe he was, and stern to view;
I knew him well, and every truant knew;
Well had the boding tremblers learn'd to trace
The day's disasters in his morning face;   200
Full well they laugh'd, with counterfeited glee,
At all his jokes, for many a joke had he;
Full well the busy whisper, circling round,
Convey'd the dismal tidings when he frown'd;
Yet he was kind; or if severe in aught,   205
The love he bore to learning was in fault;
The village all declar'd how much he knew;
'Twas certain he could write, and cypher too;
Lands he could measure, terms and tides presage,
And e'en the story ran that he could gauge.   210
In arguing too, the parson own'd his skill,
For e'en though vanquish'd, he could argue still;

While words of learned length and thund'ring sound
Amazed the gazing rustics rang'd around,
And still they gaz'd, and still the wonder grew,   215
That one small head could carry all he knew.

  But past is all his fame. The very spot
Where many a time he triumph'd, is forgot.
Near yonder thorn, that lifts its head on high,
Where once the sign-post caught the passing eye,   220
Low lies that house where nut-brown draughts inspir'd,
Where grey-beard mirth and smiling toil retir'd,
Where village statesmen talk'd with looks profound,
And news much older than their ale went round.
Imagination fondly stoops to trace   225
The parlour splendours of that festive place;
The white-wash'd wall, the nicely sanded floor,
The varnish'd clock that click'd behind the door;
The chest contriv'd a double debt to pay,
A bed by night, a chest of drawers by day;   230
The pictures plac'd for ornament and use,
The twelve good rules, the royal game of goose;
The hearth, except when winter chill'd the day,
With aspen boughs, and flowers, and fennel gay;
While broken tea-cups, wisely kept for show,   235
Rang'd o'er the chimney, glisten'd in a row.

  Vain, transitory splendours! Could not all
Reprieve the tottering mansion from its fall!
Obscure it sinks, nor shall it more impart
An hour's importance to the poor man's heart;   240
Thither no more the peasant shall repair
To sweet oblivion of his daily care;
No more the farmer's news, the barber's tale,
No more the wood-man's ballad shall prevail;
No more the smith his dusky brown shall clear,   245
Relax his pond'rous strength, and lean to hear;
The host himself no longer shall be found
Careful to see the mantling bliss go round;
Nor the coy maid, half willing to be press'd,
Shall kiss the cup to pass it to the rest.   250

  Yes! let the rich deride, the proud disdain,
These simple blessings of the lowly train;
To me more dear, congenial to my heart,
One native charm, than all the gloss of art;
Spontaneous joys, where Nature has its play,   255
The soul adopts, and owns their first-born sway;
Lightly they frolic o'er the vacant mind,

Unenvied, unmolested, unconfin'd:
But the long pomp, the midnight masquerade,
With all the freaks of wanton wealth array'd,   260
In these, ere triflers half their wish obtain,
The toiling pleasure sickens into pain;
And, e'en while fashion's brightest arts decoy,
The heart distrusting asks, if this be joy.

  Ye friends to truth, ye statesmen, who survey   265
The rich man's joys increase, the poor's decay,
'Tis yours to judge, how wide the limits stand
Between a splendid and a happy land.
Proud swells the tide with loads of freighted ore,
And shouting Folly hails them from her shore;   270
Hoards, e'en beyond the miser's wish abound,
And rich men flock from all the world around.
Yet count our gains. This wealth is but a name
That leaves our useful products still the same.
Nor so the loss. The man of wealth and pride   275
Takes up a space that many poor supplied;
Space for his lake, his park's extended bounds,
Space for his horses, equipage, and hounds;
The robe that wraps his limbs in silken sloth
Has robb'd the neighbouring fields of half their growth,   280
His seat, where solitary sports are seen,
Indignant spurns the cottage from the green;
Around the world each needful product flies,
For all the luxuries the world supplies:
While thus the land adorn'd for pleasure, all   285
In barren splendour feebly waits the fall.

  As some fair female unadorn'd and plain,
Secure to please while youth confirms her reign,
Slights every borrow'd charm that dress supplies,
Nor shares with art the triumph of her eyes: 290
But when those charms are pass'd, for charms are frail,
When time advances, and when lovers fail,
She then shines forth, solicitous to bless,
In all the glaring impotence of dress.
Thus fares the land, by luxury betray'd,   295
In nature's simplest charms at first array'd;
But verging to decline, its splendours rise,
Its vistas strike, its palaces surprise;
While scourg'd by famine from the smiling land,
The mournful peasant leads his humble band;   300
And while he sinks, without one arm to save,
The country blooms—a garden, and a grave.

Where then, ah! where, shall poverty reside,
To 'scape the pressure of continuous pride?
If to some common's fenceless limits stray'd, 305
He drives his flock to pick the scanty blade,
Those fenceless fields the sons of wealth divide,
And e'en the bare-worn common is denied.

If to the city sped—What waits him there?
To see profusion that he must not share; 310
To see ten thousand baneful arts combin'd
To pamper luxury, and thin mankind;
To see those joys the sons of pleasure know
Extorted from his fellow creature's woe.
Here, while the courtier glitters in brocade, 315
There the pale artist plies the sickly trade;
Here, while the proud their long-drawn pomps display,
There the black gibbet glooms beside the way.
The dome where Pleasure holds her midnight reign
Here, richly deck'd, admits the gorgeous train; 320
Tumultuous grandeur crowds the blazing square,
The rattling chariots clash, the torches glare.
Sure scenes like these no troubles e'er annoy!
Sure these denote one universal joy!
Are these thy serious thoughts?—Ah, turn thine eyes 325
Where the poor houseless shiv'ring female lies.
She once, perhaps, in village plenty bless'd,
Has wept at tales of innocence distress'd;
Her modest looks the cottage might adorn,
Sweet as the primrose peeps beneath the thorn; 330
Now lost to all; her friends, her virtue fled,
Near her betrayer's door she lays her head,
And, pinch'd with cold, and shrinking from the shower,
With heavy heart deplores that luckless hour,
When idly first, ambitious of the town, 335
She left her wheel and robes of country brown.

Do thine, sweet AUBURN, thine, the loveliest train,
Do thy fair tribes participate her pain?
E'en now, perhaps by cold and hunger led,
At proud men's doors they ask a little bread! 340

Ah, no. To distant climes, a dreary scene,
Where half the convex world intrudes between,
Through torrid tracts with fainting steps they go,
Where wild Altama murmurs to their woe.
Far different there from all that charm'd before, 345
The various terrors of that horrid shore;
Those blazing suns that dart a downward ray,

And fiercely shed intolerable day;
Those matted woods where birds forget to sing,
But silent bats in drowsy clusters cling; 350
Those pois'nous fields with rank luxuriance crown'd,
Where the dark scorpion gathers death around;
Where at each step the stranger fears to wake
The rattling terrors of the vengeful snake;
Where crouching tigers wait their hapless prey, 355
And savage men more murd'rous still than they;
While oft in whirls the mad tornado flies,
Mingling the ravag'd landscape with the skies.
Far different these from every former scene,
The cooling brook, the grassy-vested green, 360
The breezy covert of the warbling grove,
That only shelter'd thefts of harmless love.

  Good heaven! what sorrows gloom'd that parting day,
That call'd them from their native walks away;
When the poor exiles, every pleasure pass'd, 365
Hung round their bowers, and fondly look'd their last,
And took a long farewell, and wish'd in vain
For seats like these beyond the western main;
And shudd'ring still to face the distant deep,
Return'd and wept, and still return'd to weep. 370
The good old sire, the first prepar'd to go
To new-found worlds, and wept for others' woe;
But for himself, in conscious virtue brave,
He only wish'd for worlds beyond the grave.
His lovely daughter, lovlier in her tears, 375
The fond companion of his helpless years,
Silent went next, neglectful of her charms,
And left a lover's for a father's arms.
With louder plaints the mother spoke her woes,
And bless'd the cot where every pleasure rose 380
And kiss'd her thoughtless babes with many a tear,
And clasp'd them close, in sorrow doubly dear;
Whilst her fond husband strove to lend relief
In all the silent manliness of grief.

  O Luxury! thou curs'd by Heaven's decree, 385
How ill exchang'd are things like these for thee!
How do thy potions, with insidious joy
Diffuse their pleasures only to destroy!
Kingdoms, by thee, to sickly greatness grown,
Boast of a florid vigour not their own; 390
At every draught more large and large they grow,
A bloated mass of rank unwieldy woe;

Till sapp'd their strength, and every part unsound,
Down, down they sink, and spread a ruin round.

  E'en now the devastation is begun,   395
And half the business of destruction done;
E'en now, methinks, as pond'ring here I stand,
I see the rural virtues leave the land:
Down where yon anchoring vessel spreads the sail,
That idly waiting flaps with ev'ry gale,   400
Downward they move, a melancholy band,
Pass from the shore, and darken all the strand.
Contented toil, and hospitable care,
And kind connubial tenderness, are there;
And piety, with wishes plac'd above,   405
And steady loyalty, and faithful love.
And thou, sweet Poetry, thou loveliest maid,
Still first to fly where sensual joys invade;
Unfit in these degenerate times of shame,
To catch the heart, or strike for honest fame;   410
Dear charming nymph, neglected and decried,
My shame in crowds, my solitary pride;
Thou source of all my bliss, and all my woe,
That found'st me poor at first, and keep'st me so;
Thou guide by which the nobler arts excel,   415
Thou nurse of every virtue, fare thee well!
Farewell, and Oh! where'er thy voice be tried,
On Torno's cliffs, or Pambamarca's side,
Whether where equinoctial fervours glow,
Or winter wraps the polar world in snow,   420
Still let thy voice, prevailing over time,
Redress the rigours of th' inclement clime;
Aid slighted truth; with thy persuasive strain
Teach erring man to spurn the rage of gain;
Teach him, that states of native strength possess'd,   425
Though very poor, may still be very bless'd;
That trade's proud empire hastes to swift decay,
As ocean sweeps the labour'd mole away;
While self-dependent power can time defy,
As rocks resist the billows and the sky.   430

LYRICAL AND MISCELLANEOUS PIECES

PART OF A PROLOGUE WRITTEN AND SPOKEN BY THE POET LABERIUS

A ROMAN KNIGHT, WHOM CAESAR FORCED UPON THE STAGE

PRESERVED BY MACROBIUS.

WHAT! no way left to shun th' inglorious stage,
And save from infamy my sinking age!
Scarce half alive, oppress'd with many a year,
What in the name of dotage drives me here?
A time there was, when glory was my guide,   5
Nor force nor fraud could turn my steps aside;
Unaw'd by pow'r, and unappall'd by fear,
With honest thrift I held my honour dear;
But this vile hour disperses all my store,
And all my hoard of honour is no more.   10
For ah! too partial to my life's decline,
Caesar persuades, submission must be mine;
Him I obey, whom heaven itself obeys,
Hopeless of pleasing, yet inclin'd to please.
Here then at once, I welcome every shame,   15
And cancel at threescore a life of fame;
No more my titles shall my children tell,
The old buffoon will fit my name as well;
This day beyond its term my fate extends,
For life is ended when our honour ends.   20

ON A BEAUTIFUL YOUTH STRUCK BLIND WITH LIGHTNING

(Imitated from the Spanish.)

SURE 'twas by Providence design'd,
  Rather in pity, than in hate,
That he should be, like Cupid, blind,
  To save him from Narcissus' fate.

THE GIFT TO IRIS, IN BOW STREET
CONVENT GARDEN

Say, cruel Iris, pretty rake,
  Dear mercenary beauty,
What annual offering shall I make,
  Expressive of my duty?

My heart, a victim to thine eyes,   5
  Should I at once deliver,
Say, would the angry fair one prize
  The gift, who slights the giver?

A bill, a jewel, watch, or toy,
  My rivals give—and let 'em;   10
If gems, or gold, impart a joy,
  I'll give them—when I get 'em.

I'll give—but not the full-blown rose,
  Or rose-bud more in fashion;
Such short-liv'd offerings but disclose   15
  A transitory passion.

I'll give thee something yet unpaid,
  Not less sincere, than civil:
I'll give thee—Ah! too charming maid,
  I'll give thee—To the devil.   30

THE LOGICIANS REFUTED
IN IMITATION OF DEAN SWIFT

Logicians have but ill defin'd
As rational, the human kind;
Reason, they say, belongs to man,
But let them prove it if they can.
Wise Aristotle and Smiglecius,   5
By ratiocinations specious,
Have strove to prove with great precision,
With definition and division,
Homo est ratione praeditum,—
But for my soul I cannot credit 'em;   10
And must in spite of them maintain,
That man and all his ways are vain;
And that this boasted lord of nature
Is both a weak and erring creature;
That instinct is a surer guide   15

Than reason-boasting mortals' pride;
And that brute beasts are far before 'em,
Deus est anima brutorum.
Who ever knew an honest brute
At law his neighbour prosecute, 20
Bring action for assault and battery,
Or friend beguile with lies and flattery?
O'er plains they ramble unconfin'd,
No politics disturb their mind;
They eat their meals, and take their sport, 25
Nor know who's in or out at court;
They never to the levee go
To treat as dearest friend, a foe;
They never importune his grace,
Nor ever cringe to men in place; 30
Nor undertake a dirty job,
Nor draw the quill to write for B——b.
Fraught with invective they ne'er go
To folks at Pater-Noster-Row;
No judges, fiddlers, dancing-masters, 35
No pick-pockets, or poetasters,
Are known to honest quadrupeds;
No single brute his fellow leads.
Brutes never meet in bloody fray,
Nor cut each others' throats, for pay. 40
Of beasts, it is confess'd, the ape
Comes nearest us in human shape;
Like man he imitates each fashion,
And malice is his ruling passion;
But both in malice and grimaces 45
A courtier any ape surpasses.
Behold him humbly cringing wait
Upon a minister of state;
View him soon after to inferiors,
Aping the conduct of superiors; 50
He promises with equal air,
And to perform takes equal care.
He in his turn finds imitators;
At court, the porters, lacqueys, waiters,
Their master's manners still contract, 55
And footmen, lords and dukes can act.
Thus at the court both great an small
Behave alike—for all ape all.

A SONNET

Weeping, murmuring, complaining,
  Lost to every gay delight;
Myra, too sincere for feigning,
  Fears th' approaching bridal night.

Yet, why impair thy bright perfection?   5
  Or dim thy beauty with a tear?
Had Myra followed my direction,
  She long had wanted cause of fear.

STANZAS ON THE TAKING OF QUEBEC
AND DEATH
OF GENERAL WOLFE

Amidst the clamour of exulting joys,
  Which triumph forces from the patriot heart,
Grief dares to mingle her soul-piercing voice,
  And quells the raptures which from pleasures start.

O Wolfe! to thee a streaming flood of woe,   5
  Sighing we pay, and think e'en conquest dear;
Quebec in vain shall teach our breast to glow,
  Whilst thy sad fate extorts the heart-wrung tear.

Alive the foe thy dreadful vigour fled,
  And saw thee fall with joy-pronouncing eyes: 10
Yet they shall know thou conquerest, though dead—
  Since from thy tomb a thousand heroes rise!

AN ELEGY ON THAT GLORY OF HER SEX,
MRS. MARY BLAIZE

Good people all, with one accord,
  Lament for Madam Blaize,
Who never wanted a good word—
  From those who spoke her praise.

The needy seldom pass'd her door,   5
  And always found her kind;
She freely lent to all the poor,—
  Who left a pledge behind.

She strove the neighbourhood to please,
  With manners wond'rous winning,   10
And never follow'd wicked ways,—

Unless when she was sinning.

At church, in silks and satins new,
   With hoop of monstrous size,
She never slumber'd in her pew,—   15
But when she shut her eyes.

Her love was sought, I do aver,
   By twenty beaux and more;
The king himself has follow'd her,—
When she has walk'd before.   20

But now her wealth and finery fled,
   Her hangers-on cut short all;
The doctors found, when she was dead,—
Her last disorder mortal.

Let us lament, in sorrow sore,   25
   For Kent-street well may say,
That had she liv'd a twelve-month more,—
She had not died to-day.

DESCRIPTION OF AN AUTHOR'S BEDCHAMBER

Where the Red Lion flaring o'er the way,
Invites each passing stranger that can pay;
Where Calvert's butt, and Parsons' black champagne,
Regale the drabs and bloods of Drury-lane;
There in a lonely room, from bailiffs snug,   5
The Muse found Scroggen stretch'd beneath a rug;
A window, patch'd with paper, lent a ray,
That dimly show'd the state in which he lay;
The sanded floor that grits beneath the tread;
The humid wall with paltry pictures spread: 10
The royal game of goose was there in view,
And the twelve rules the royal martyr drew;
The seasons, fram'd with listing, found a place,
And brave prince William show'd his lamp-black face:
The morn was cold, he views with keen desire   15
The rusty grate unconscious of a fire;
With beer and milk arrears the frieze was scor'd,
And five crack'd teacups dress'd the chimney board;
A nightcap deck'd his brows instead of bay,
A cap by night—a stocking all the day!   20

ON SEEING MRS. ** PERFORM IN THE CHARACTER OF ****

For you, bright fair, the nine address their lays,
And tune my feeble voice to sing thy praise.
The heartfelt power of every charm divine,
Who can withstand their all-commanding shine?
See how she moves along with every grace,   5
While soul-brought tears steal down each shining face.
She speaks! 'tis rapture all, and nameless bliss,
Ye gods! what transport e'er compared to this.
As when in Paphian groves the Queen of Love
With fond complaint addressed the listening Jove,   10
'Twas joy, and endless blisses all around,
And rocks forgot their hardness at the sound.
Then first, at last even Jove was taken in,
And felt her charms, without disguise, within.

OF THE DEATH OF THE LEFT HON. ***

Ye Muses, pour the pitying tear
  For Pollio snatch'd away;
O! had he liv'd another year!—
  He had not died to-day.

O! were he born to bless mankind,   5
  In virtuous times of yore,
Heroes themselves had fallen behind!—
  Whene'er he went before.

How sad the groves and plains appear,
  And sympathetic sheep;   10
Even pitying hills would drop a tear!—
  If hills could learn to weep.

His bounty in exalted strain
  Each bard might well display;
Since none implor'd relief in vain!—   15
  That went reliev'd away.

And hark! I hear the tuneful throng
  His obsequies forbid,
He still shall live, shall live as long!—
  As ever dead man did.   20

AN EPIGRAM
ADDRESSED TO THE GENTLEMEN REFLECTED ON IN THE ROSCIAD, A POEM, BY THE AUTHOR

Worried with debts and past all hopes of bail,
His pen he prostitutes t' avoid a gaol.
                    ROSCOM.

> Let not the *hungry* Bavius' angry stroke
> Awake resentment, or your rage provoke;
> But pitying his distress, let virtue shine,
> And giving each your bounty, *let him dine*;
> For thus retain'd, as learned counsel can,   5
> Each case, however bad, he'll new japan;
> And by a quick transition, plainly show
> 'Twas no defect of yours, but *pocket low*,
> That caused his *putrid kennel* to o'erflow.

TO G. C. AND R. L.

'Twas you, or I, or he, or all together,
'Twas one, both, three of them, they know not whether;
This, I believe, between us great or small,
You, I, he, wrote it not—'twas Churchill's all.

TRANSLATION OF A SOUTH AMERICAN ODE

> In all my Enna's beauties blest,
>   Amidst profusion still I pine;
> For though she gives me up her breast,
>   Its panting tenant is not mine.

THE DOUBLE TRANSFORMATION A TALE

Secluded from domestic strife,
Jack Book-worm led a college life;
A fellowship at twenty-five
Made him the happiest man alive;
He drank his glass and crack'd his joke,   5
And freshmen wonder'd as he spoke.

  Such pleasures, unalloy'd with care,
Could any accident impair?
Could Cupid's shaft at length transfix
Our swain, arriv'd at thirty-six?   10
O had the archer ne'er come down
To ravage in a country town!
Or Flavia been content to stop
At triumphs in a Fleet-street shop.

O had her eyes forgot to blaze!   15
Or Jack had wanted eyes to gaze.
O!——But let exclamation cease,
Her presence banish'd all his peace.
So with decorum all things carried;
Miss frown'd, and blush'd, and then was—married. 20

 Need we expose to vulgar sight
The raptures of the bridal night?
Need we intrude on hallow'd ground,
Or draw the curtains clos'd around?
Let it suffice, that each had charms; 25
He clasp'd a goddess in his arms;
And though she felt his usage rough,
Yet in a man 'twas well enough.

 The honey-moon like lightning flew,
The second brought its transports too. 30
A third, a fourth, were not amiss,
The fifth was friendship mix'd with bliss:
But when a twelvemonth pass'd away,
Jack found his goddess made of clay;
Found half the charms that deck'd her face 35
Arose from powder, shreds, or lace;
But still the worst remain'd behind,
That very face had robb'd her mind.

 Skill'd in no other arts was she
But dressing, patching, repartee; 40
And, just as humour rose or fell,
By turns a slattern or a belle;
'Tis true she dress'd with modern grace,
Half naked at a ball or race;
But when at home, at board or bed, 45
Five greasy nightcaps wrapp'd her head.
Could so much beauty condescend
To be a dull domestic friend?
Could any curtain-lectures bring
To decency so fine a thing? 50
In short, by night, 'twas fits or fretting;
By day, 'twas gadding or coquetting.
Fond to be seen, she kept a bevy
Of powder'd coxcombs at her levy;
The 'squire and captain took their stations, 55
And twenty other near relations;
Jack suck'd his pipe, and often broke
A sigh in suffocating smoke;
While all their hours were pass'd between

Insulting repartee or spleen.   60

  Thus as her faults each day were known,
He thinks her features coarser grown;
He fancies every vice she shows,
Or thins her lip, or points her nose:
Whenever rage or envy rise,   65
How wide her mouth, how wild her eyes!
He knows not how, but so it is,
Her face is grown a knowing phiz;
And, though her fops are wond'rous civil,
He thinks her ugly as the devil.   70

  Now, to perplex the ravell'd noose,
As each a different way pursues,
While sullen or loquacious strife,
Promis'd to hold them on for life,
That dire disease, whose ruthless power   75
Withers the beauty's transient flower:
Lo! the small-pox, whose horrid glare
Levell'd its terrors at the fair;
And, rifling ev'ry youthful grace,
Left but the remnant of a face.   80

  The glass, grown hateful to her sight,
Reflected now a perfect fright:
Each former art she vainly tries
To bring back lustre to her eyes.
In vain she tries her paste and creams,   85
To smooth her skin, or hide its seams;
Her country beaux and city cousins,
Lovers no more, flew off by dozens:
The 'squire himself was seen to yield,
And e'en the captain quit the field.   90

  Poor Madam, now condemn'd to hack
The rest of life with anxious Jack,
Perceiving others fairly flown,
Attempted pleasing him alone.
Jack soon was dazzl'd to behold   95
Her present face surpass the old;
With modesty her cheeks are dy'd,
Humility displaces pride;
For tawdry finery is seen
A person ever neatly clean: 100
No more presuming on her sway,
She learns good-nature every day;
Serenely gay, and strict in duty,

Jack finds his wife a perfect beauty.

A NEW SIMILE IN THE MANNER OF SWIFT

Long had I sought in vain to find
A likeness for the scribbling kind;
The modern scribbling kind, who write
In wit, and sense, and nature's spite:
Till reading, I forget what day on, 5
A chapter out of Tooke's Pantheon,
I think I met with something there,
To suit my purpose to a hair;
But let us not proceed too furious,
First please to turn to god Mercurius; 10
You'll find him pictur'd at full length
In book the second, page the tenth:
The stress of all my proofs on him I lay,
And now proceed we to our simile.

 Imprimis, pray observe his hat, 15
Wings upon either side—mark that.
Well! what is it from thence we gather?
Why these denote a brain of feather.
A brain of feather! very right,
With wit that's flighty, learning light; 20
Such as to modern bard's decreed:
A just comparison,—proceed.

 In the next place, his feet peruse,
Wings grow again from both his shoes;
Design'd, no doubt, their part to bear, 25
And waft his godship through the air;
And here my simile unites,
For in a modern poet's flights,
I'm sure it may be justly said,
His feet are useful as his head. 30

 Lastly, vouchsafe t'observe his hand,
Filled with a snake-encircl'd wand;
By classic authors term'd caduceus,
And highly fam'd for several uses.
To wit—most wond'rously endu'd, 35
No poppy water half so good;
For let folks only get a touch,
Its soporific virtue's such,
Though ne'er so much awake before,
That quickly they begin to snore. 40
Add too, what certain writers tell,

With this he drives men's souls to hell.

  Now to apply, begin we then;
His wand's a modern author's pen;
The serpents round about it twin'd   45
Denote him of the reptile kind;
Denote the rage with which he writes,
His frothy slaver, venom'd bites;
An equal semblance still to keep,
Alike too both conduce to sleep.   50
This diff'rence only, as the god
Drove souls to Tart'rus with his rod,
With his goosequill the scribbling elf,
Instead of others, damns himself.

  And here my simile almost tript,   55
Yet grant a word by way of postscript.
Moreover, Merc'ry had a failing:
Well! what of that? out with it—stealing;
In which all modern bards agree,
Being each as great a thief as he: 60
But ev'n this deity's existence
Shall lend my simile assistance.
Our modern bards! why what a pox
Are they but senseless stones and blocks?

EDWIN AND ANGELINA A BALLAD

  'Turn, gentle hermit of the dale,
    And guide my lonely way,
  To where yon taper cheers the vale
    With hospitable ray.

  'For here, forlorn and lost I tread,   5
    With fainting steps and slow;
  Where wilds immeasurably spread,
    Seem length'ning as I go.'

  'Forbear, my son,' the hermit cries,
    'To tempt the dangerous gloom;   10
  For yonder faithless phantom flies
    To lure thee to thy doom.

  'Here to the houseless child of want
    My door is open still;
  And though my portion is but scant,   15
    I give it with good will.

'Then turn to-night, and freely share
   Whate'er my cell bestows;
My rushy couch, and frugal fare,
   My blessing and repose.   20

'No flocks that range the valley free
   To slaughter I condemn:
Taught by that power that pities me,
   I learn to pity them.

'But from the mountain's grassy side   25
   A guiltless feast I bring;
A scrip with herbs and fruits supplied,
   And water from the spring.

'Then, pilgrim, turn, thy cares forgo;
   All earth-born cares are wrong: 30
Man wants but little here below,
   Nor wants that little long.'

Soft as the dew from heav'n descends,
   His gentle accents fell:
The modest stranger lowly bends,   35
   And follows to the cell.

Far in a wilderness obscure
   The lonely mansion lay;
A refuge to the neighbouring poor
   And strangers led astray.   40

No stores beneath its humble thatch
   Requir'd a master's care;
The wicket, opening with a latch,
   Receiv'd the harmless pair.

And now, when busy crowds retire   45
   To take their evening rest,
The hermit trimm'd his little fire,
   And cheer'd his pensive guest:

And spread his vegetable store,
   And gaily press'd, and smil'd;   50
And, skill'd in legendary lore,
   The lingering hours beguil'd.

Around in sympathetic mirth
   Its tricks the kitten tries;

The cricket chirrups in the hearth;   55
  The crackling faggot flies.

But nothing could a charm impart
  To soothe the stranger's woe;
For grief was heavy at his heart,
  And tears began to flow.   60

His rising cares the hermit spied,
  With answ'ring care oppress'd;
'And whence, unhappy youth,' he cried,
  'The sorrows of thy breast?

'From better habitations spurn'd,   65
  Reluctant dost thou rove;
Or grieve for friendship unreturn'd,
  Or unregarded love?

'Alas! the joys that fortune brings
  Are trifling, and decay;   70
And those who prize the paltry things,
  More trifling still than they.

'And what is friendship but a name,
  A charm that lulls to sleep;
A shade that follows wealth or fame,   75
  But leaves the wretch to weep?

'And love is still an emptier sound,
  The modern fair one's jest:
On earth unseen, or only found
  To warm the turtle's nest.   80

'For shame, fond youth, thy sorrows hush,
  And spurn the sex,' he said:
But, while he spoke, a rising blush
  His love-lorn guest betray'd.

Supris'd, he sees new beauties rise,   85
  Swift mantling to the view;
Like colours o'er the morning skies,
  As bright, as transient too.

The bashful look, the rising breast,
  Alternate spread alarms: 90
The lovely stranger stands confess'd
  A maid in all her charms.

'And, ah! forgive a stranger rude,
   A wretch forlorn,' she cried;
'Whose feet unhallow'd thus intrude   95
   Where heaven and you reside.

'But let a maid thy pity share,
   Whom love has taught to stray;
Who seeks for rest, but finds despair
   Companion of her way.   100

'My father liv'd beside the Tyne,
   A wealthy lord was he;
And all his wealth was mark'd as mine,
   He had but only me.

'To win me from his tender arms   105
   Unnumber'd suitors came;
Who prais'd me for imputed charms,
   And felt or feign'd a flame.

Each hour a mercenary crowd
   With richest proffers strove: 110
Amongst the rest young Edwin bow'd,
   But never talk'd of love.

'In humble, simplest habit clad,
   No wealth nor power had he;
Wisdom and worth were all he had,   115
   But these were all to me.

'And when beside me in the dale
   He caroll'd lays of love;
His breath lent fragrance to the gale,
   And music to the grove.   120

'The blossom opening to the day,
   The dews of heaven refin'd,
Could nought of purity display,
   To emulate his mind.

'The dew, the blossom on the tree,   125
   With charms inconstant shine;
Their charms were his, but woe to me!
   Their constancy was mine.

'For still I tried each fickle art,
   Importunate and vain: 130
And while his passion touch'd my heart,

    I triumph'd in his pain.

'Till quite dejected with my scorn,
    He left me to my pride;
And sought a solitude forlorn, 135
    In secret, where he died.

'But mine the sorrow, mine the fault,
    And well my life shall pay;
I'll seek the solitude he sought,
    And stretch me where he lay. 140

'And there forlorn, despairing, hid,
    I'll lay me down and die;
'Twas so for me that Edwin did,
    And so for him will I.'

'Forbid it, heaven!' the hermit cried, 145
    And clasp'd her to his breast:
The wondering fair one turn'd to chide,
    'Twas Edwin's self that prest.

'Turn, Angelina, ever dear,
    My charmer, turn to see 150
Thy own, thy long-lost Edwin here,
    Restor'd to love and thee.

'Thus let me hold thee to my heart,
    And ev'ry care resign;
And shall we never, never part, 155
    My life—my all that's mine?

'No, never from this hour to part,
    We'll live and love so true;
The sigh that rends thy constant heart
    Shall break thy Edwin's too.' 160

ELEGY ON THE DEATH OF A MAD DOG

Good people all, of every sort,
    Give ear unto my song;
And if you find it wond'rous short,
    It cannot hold you long.

In Islington there was a man, 5
    Of whom the world might say,
That still a godly race he ran,

    Whene'er he went to pray.

A kind and gentle heart he had,
  To comfort friends and foes;   10
The naked every day he clad,
  When he put on his clothes.

And in that town a dog was found,
  As many dogs there be,
Both mongrel, puppy, whelp, and hound,   15
  And curs of low degree.

This dog and man at first were friends;
  But when a pique began,
The dog, to gain some private ends,
  Went mad and bit the man.   20

Around from all the neighbouring streets
  The wond'ring neighbours ran,
And swore the dog had lost his wits,
  To bite so good a man.

The wound it seem'd both sore and sad   25
  To every Christian eye;
And while they swore the dog was mad,
  They swore the man would die.

But soon a wonder came to light,
  That show'd the rogues they lied: 30
The man recover'd of the bite,
  The dog it was that died.

SONG FROM 'THE VICAR OF WAKEFIELD'

When lovely woman stoops to folly,
  And finds too late that men betray,
What charm can soothe her melancholy,
  What art can wash her guilt away?

The only art her guilt to cover,   5
  To hide her shame from every eye,
To give repentance to her lover,
  And wring his bosom, is—to die.

EPILOGUE TO 'THE GOOD NATUR'D MAN'

As puffing quacks some caitiff wretch procure
To swear the pill, or drop, has wrought a cure;
Thus on the stage, our play-wrights still depend
For Epilogues and Prologues on some friend,
Who knows each art of coaxing up the town,   5
And make full many a bitter pill go down.
Conscious of this, our bard has gone about,
And teas'd each rhyming friend to help him out.
'An Epilogue—things can't go on without it;
It could not fail, would you but set about it.'   10
'Young man,' cries one—a bard laid up in clover—
'Alas, young man, my writing days are over;
Let boys play tricks, and kick the straw; not I:
Your brother Doctor there, perhaps, may try.'
'What I? dear Sir,' the Doctor interposes   15
'What plant my thistle, Sir, among his roses!
No, no; I've other contests to maintain;
To-night I head our troops at Warwick Lane:
Go, ask your manager.' 'Who, me? Your pardon;
Those things are not our forte at Covent Garden.'   20
Our Author's friends, thus plac'd at happy distance,
Give him good words indeed, but no assistance.
As some unhappy wight, at some new play,
At the Pit door stands elbowing a way,
While oft, with many a smile, and many a shrug,   25
He eyes the centre, where his friends sit snug;
His simp'ring friends, with pleasure in their eyes,
Sink as he sinks, and as he rises rise;
He nods, they nod; he cringes, they grimace;
But not a soul will budge to give him place.   30
Since then, unhelp'd, our bard must now conform
'To 'bide the pelting of this pitiless storm'—
Blame where you must, be candid where you can;
And be each critic the *Good Natur'd Man*.

EPILOGUE TO 'THE SISTER'

WHAT! five long acts—and all to make us wiser!
Our authoress sure has wanted an adviser.
Had she consulted *me*, she should have made
Her moral play a speaking masquerade;
Warm'd up each bustling scene, and in her rage   5
Have emptied all the green-room on the stage.
My life on't, this had kept her play from sinking;
Have pleas'd our eyes, and sav'd the pain of thinking.

Well! since she thus has shown her want of skill,
What if I give a masquerade?—I will.   10
But how? ay, there's the rub! (*pausing*)—I've got my cue:
The world's a masquerade! the maskers, you, you, you.
            (*To Boxes, Pit, and Gallery.*)
——, what a group the motley scene discloses!
False wits, false wives, false virgins, and false spouses!
Statesmen with bridles on; and, close beside 'em,   15
Patriots, in party-coloured suits, that ride 'em.
There Hebes, turn'd of fifty, try once more
To raise a flame in Cupids of threescore.
These in their turn, with appetites as keen,
Deserting fifty, fasten on fifteen,   20
Miss, not yet full fifteen, with fire uncommon,
Flings down her sampler, and takes up the woman:
The little urchin smiles, and spreads her lure,
And tries to kill, ere she's got power to cure.
Thus 'tis with all—their chief and constant care   25
Is to seem everything but what they are.
Yon broad, bold, angry spark, I fix my eye on,
Who seems to have robb'd his vizor from the lion;
Who frowns, and talks, and swears, with round parade,
Looking as who should say, D——! who's afraid?   30
            (*Mimicking*)

Strip but his vizor off, and sure I am
You'll find his lionship a very lamb.
Yon politician, famous in debate,
Perhaps, to vulgar eyes, bestrides the state;
Yet, when he deigns his real shape t' assume,   35
He turns old woman, and bestrides a broom.
Yon patriot, too, who presses on your sight,
And seems to every gazer all in white,
If with a bribe his candour you attack,
He bows, turns round, and whip—the man's a black!   40
Yon critic, too—but whither do I run?
If I proceed, our bard will be undone!
Well then a truce, since she requests it too:
Do you spare her, and I'll for once spare you.

PROLOGUE TO 'ZOBEIDE'

In these bold times, when Learning's sons explore
The distant climate and the savage shore;
When wise Astronomers to India steer,
And quit for Venus, many a brighter here;
While Botanists, all cold to smiles and dimpling,   5

Forsake the fair, and patiently—go simpling;
When every bosom swells with wond'rous scenes,
Priests, cannibals, and hoity-toity queens:
Our bard into the general spirit enters,
And fits his little frigate for adventures: 10
With Scythian stores, and trinkets deeply laden,
He this way steers his course, in hopes of trading—
Yet ere he lands he 'as ordered me before,
To make an observation on the shore.
Where are we driven? our reck'ning sure is lost!   15
This seems a barren and a dangerous coast.
—— what a sultry climate am I under!
Yon ill foreboding cloud seems big with thunder.
        (*Upper Gallery.*)
There Mangroves spread, and larger than I've seen 'em—
        (*Pit.*)
Here trees of stately size—and turtles in 'em—   20
        (*Balconies.*)
Here ill-condition'd oranges abound—
        (*Stage.*)
And apples (*takes up one and tastes it*), bitter apples
 strew the ground.
The place is uninhabited, I fear!
I heard a hissing—there are serpents here!
O there the natives are—a dreadful race!   25
The men have tails, the women paint the face!
No doubt they're all barbarians.—Yes, 'tis so,
I'll try to make palaver with them though;
        (*Making signs.*)
'Tis best, however, keeping at a distance.
Good Savages, our Captain craves assistance;   30
Our ship's well stor'd;—in yonder creek we've laid her;
His honour is no mercenary trader;
This is his first adventure; lend him aid,
Or you may chance to spoil a thriving trade.
His goods, he hopes are prime, and brought from far,   35
Equally fit for gallantry and war.
What! no reply to promises so ample?
I'd best step back—and order up a sample.

THRENODIA AUGUSTALIS

SACRED TO THE MEMORY OF HER LATE ROYAL HIGHNESS THE PRINCESS DOWAGER OF WALES.

OVERTURE—A SOLEMN DIRGE. AIR—TRIO.

ARISE, ye sons of worth, arise,
  And waken every note of woe;
When truth and virtue reach the skies,
  'Tis ours to weep the want below!

CHORUS.

When truth and virtue, etc.   5

MAN SPEAKER.

The praise attending pomp and power,
  The incense given to kings,
Are but the trappings of an hour—
  Mere transitory things!
The base bestow them: but the good agree   10
To spurn the venal gifts as flattery.
  But when to pomp and power are join'd
  An equal dignity of mind—
When titles are the smallest claim—
  When wealth and rank and noble blood,   15
  But aid the power of doing good—
Then all their trophies last; and flattery turns to fame.

  Bless'd spirit thou, whose fame, just born to bloom
Shall spread and flourish from the tomb,
  How hast thou left mankind for heaven!   20
Even now reproach and faction mourn.
And, wondering how their rage was borne,
  Request to be forgiven.
Alas! they never had thy hate:
  Unmov'd in conscious rectitude,   25
  Thy towering mind self-centred stood,
Nor wanted man's opinion to be great.
In vain, to charm thy ravish'd sight,
  A thousand gifts would fortune send;
  In vain, to drive thee from the right,   30
  A thousand sorrows urg'd thy end:
Like some well-fashion'd arch thy patience stood,
And purchas'd strength from its increasing load.
Pain met thee like a friend that set thee free;
Affliction still is virtue's opportunity!   35

Virtue, on herself relying,
  Ev'ry passion hush'd to rest,
Loses ev'ry pain of dying
  In the hopes of being blest.
Ev'ry added pang she suffers   40
  Some increasing good bestows,
Ev'ry shock that malice offers
  Only rocks her to repose.

SONG. BY A MAN—AFFETTUOSO.

Virtue, on herself relying,
  Ev'ry passion hush'd to rest,   45
Loses ev'ry pain of dying
  In the hopes of being blest.

Ev'ry added pang she suffers
  Some increasing good bestows,
Ev'ry shock that malice offers,   50
  Only rocks her to repose.

WOMAN SPEAKER.

Yet, ah! what terrors frowned upon her fate—
  Death, with its formidable band,
Fever and pain and pale consumptive care,
  Determin'd took their stand: 55
Nor did the cruel ravagers design
  To finish all their efforts at a blow;
  But, mischievously slow,
They robb'd the relic and defac'd the shrine.
  With unavailing grief,   60
  Despairing of relief,
Her weeping children round
  Beheld each hour
  Death's growing power,
And trembled as he frown'd.   65

As helpless friends who view from shore
The labouring ship, and hear the tempest roar,
  While winds and waves their wishes cross—
They stood, while hope and comfort fail,
Not to assist, but to bewail   70
  The inevitable loss.
Relentless tyrant, at thy call
  How do the good, the virtuous fall!
Truth, beauty, worth, and all that most engage,
But wake thy vengeance and provoke thy rage.   75

SONG. BY A MAN.—BASSO.—STACCATO.—SPIRITOSO.

When vice my dart and scythe supply,
How great a king of terrors I!
If folly, fraud, your hearts engage,
Tremble, ye mortals, at my rage!
Fall, round me fall, ye little things, 80
Ye statesmen, warriors, poets, kings;
If virtue fail her counsel sage,
Tremble, ye mortals, at my rage!

MAN SPEAKER.

Yet let that wisdom, urged by her example,
Teach us to estimate what all must suffer; 85
Let us prize death as the best gift of nature—
As a safe inn, where weary travellers,
When they have journeyed through a world of cares,
May put off life and be at rest for ever.
Groans, weeping friends, indeed, and gloomy sables, 90
May oft distract us with their sad solemnity:
The preparation is the executioner.
Death, when unmasked, shows me a friendly face,
And is a terror only at a distance;
For as the line of life conducts me on 95
To Death's great court, the prospect seems more fair.
'Tis Nature's kind retreat, that's always open
To take us in when we have drained the cup
Of life, or worn our days to wretchedness.
 In that secure, serene retreat, 100
  Where all the humble, all the great,
   Promiscuously recline;
  Where wildly huddled to the eye,
  The beggar's pouch and prince's purple lie,
   May every bliss be thine. 105
And ah! bless'd spirit, wheresoe'er thy flight,
Through rolling worlds, or fields of liquid light,
May cherubs welcome their expected guest;
May saints with songs receive thee to their rest;
May peace that claimed while here thy warmest love, 110
May blissful endless peace be thine above!

SONG. BY A WOMAN.—AMOROSO.

Lovely, lasting Peace below,
Comforter of every woe,
Heav'nly born, and bred on high,
To crown the favourites of the sky— 115
Lovely, lasting Peace, appear;

This world itself, if thou art here,
Is once again with Eden blest,
And man contains it in his breast.

WOMAN SPEAKER.

Our vows are heard! Long, long to mortal eyes, 120
Her soul was fitting to its kindred skies:
Celestial-like her bounty fell,
Where modest want and patient sorrow dwell;
Want pass'd for merit at her door,
  Unseen the modest were supplied, 125
Her constant pity fed the poor—
  Then only poor, indeed, the day she died.
And oh! for this! while sculpture decks thy shrine,
  And art exhausts profusion round,
The tribute of a tear be mine, 130
  A simple song, a sigh profound.
There Faith shall come, a pilgrim gray,
To bless the tomb that wraps thy clay;
And calm Religion shall repair
To dwell a weeping hermit there. 135
Truth, Fortitude, and Friendship shall agree
To blend their virtues while they think of thee.

AIR. CHORUS.—POMPOSO.

Let us, let all the world agree,
To profit by resembling thee.

PART II

OVERTURE—PASTORALE

MAN SPEAKER.

Fast by that shore where Thames' translucent stream
  Reflects new glories on his breast,
Where, splendid as the youthful poet's dream,
  He forms a scene beyond Elysium blest—
Where sculptur'd elegance and native grace 5
Unite to stamp the beauties of the place,
  While sweetly blending still are seen
  The wavy lawn, the sloping green—
While novelty, with cautious cunning,
Through ev'ry maze of fancy running, 10
  From China borrows aid to deck the scene—
There, sorrowing by the river's glassy bed,
  Forlorn, a rural bard complain'd,

All whom Augusta's bounty fed,
  All whom her clemency sustain'd;   15
The good old sire, unconscious of decay,
The modest matron, clad in homespun gray,
The military boy, the orphan'd maid,
The shatter'd veteran, now first dismay'd;
These sadly join beside the murmuring deep,   20
    And, as they view
    The towers of Kew,
Call on their mistress—now no more—and weep.

CHORUS.—AFFETTUOSO.—LARGO.

Ye shady walks, ye waving greens,
Ye nodding towers, ye fairy scenes—   25
Let all your echoes now deplore
That she who form'd your beauties is no more.

MAN SPEAKER.

First of the train the patient rustic came,
  Whose callous hand had form'd the scene,
Bending at once with sorrow and with age,   30
  With many a tear and many a sigh between;
'And where,' he cried, 'shall now my babes have bread,
  Or how shall age support its feeble fire?
No lord will take me now, my vigour fled,
  Nor can my strength perform what they require; 35
Each grudging master keeps the labourer bare—
A sleek and idle race is all their care.
My noble mistress thought not so:
  Her bounty, like the morning dew,
Unseen, though constant, used to flow;   40
  And as my strength decay'd, her bounty grew.'

WOMAN SPEAKER.

In decent dress, and coarsely clean,
The pious matron next was seen—
Clasp'd in her hand a godly book was borne,
By use and daily meditation worn;   45
That decent dress, this holy guide,
Augusta's care had well supplied.
'And ah!' she cries, all woe-begone,
  'What now remains for me?
Oh! where shall weeping want repair,   50
  To ask for charity?
Too late in life for me to ask,
  And shame prevents the deed,

And tardy, tardy are the times
  To succour, should I need. 55
But all my wants, before I spoke,
  Were to my Mistress known;
She still reliev'd, nor sought my praise,
  Contented with her own.
But ev'ry day her name I'll bless, 60
  My morning prayer, my evening song,
I'll praise her while my life shall last,
  A life that cannot last me long.'

SONG. BY A WOMAN.

Each day, each hour, her name I'll bless—
  My morning and my evening song; 65
And when in death my vows shall cease,
  My children shall the note prolong.

MAN SPEAKER.

The hardy veteran after struck the sight,
  Scarr'd, mangled, maim'd in every part,
Lopp'd of his limbs in many a gallant fight, 70
  In nought entire—except his heart.
Mute for a while, and sullenly distress'd,
At last the impetuous sorrow fir'd his breast.
  'Wild is the whirlwind rolling
    O'er Afric's sandy plain, 75
  And wild the tempest howling
    Along the billow'd main:
  But every danger felt before—
  The raging deep, the whirlwind's roar—
  Less dreadful struck me with dismay, 80
  Than what I feel this fatal day.
Oh, let me fly a land that spurns the brave,
Oswego's dreary shores shall be my grave;
I'll seek that less inhospitable coast,
And lay my body where my limbs were lost.' 85

SONG. BY A MAN.—BASSO. SPIRITOSO.

  Old Edward's sons, unknown to yield,
Shall crowd from Crecy's laurell'd field,
  To do thy memory right;
For thine and Britain's wrongs they feel,
Again they snatch the gleamy steel, 90
  And wish the avenging fight.

WOMAN SPEAKER.

 In innocence and youth complaining,
  Next appear'd a lovely maid,
 Affliction o'er each feature reigning,
  Kindly came in beauty's aid;   95
 Every grace that grief dispenses,
  Every glance that warms the soul,
 In sweet succession charmed the senses,
  While pity harmonized the whole.
'The garland of beauty'—'tis thus she would say— 100
 'No more shall my crook or my temples adorn,
I'll not wear a garland—Augusta's away,
 I'll not wear a garland until she return;
But alas! that return I never shall see,
 The echoes of Thames shall my sorrows proclaim, 105
There promised a lover to come—but, O me!
 'Twas death,—'twas the death of my mistress that came.
But ever, for ever, her image shall last,
 I'll strip all the spring of its earliest bloom;
On her grave shall the cowslip and primrose be cast, 110
 And the new-blossomed thorn shall whiten her tomb.'

SONG. BY A WOMAN.—PASTORALE.

With garlands of beauty the queen of the May
 No more will her crook or her temples adorn;
For who'd wear a garland when she is away,
 When she is remov'd, and shall never return. 115

On the grave of Augusta these garlands be plac'd,
 We'll rifle the spring of its earliest bloom,
And there shall the cowslip and primrose be cast,
 And the new-blossom'd thorn shall whiten her tomb.

CHORUS.—ALTRO MODO.

On the grave of Augusta this garland be plac'd, 120
 We'll rifle the spring of its earliest bloom,
And there shall the cowslip and primrose be cast,
 And the tears of her country shall water her tomb.

SONG FROM 'SHE STOOPS TO CONQUER'

Let school-masters puzzle their brain,
 With grammar, and nonsense, and learning;
Good liquor, I stoutly maintain,
 Gives 'genus' a better discerning.
Let them brag of their heathenish gods, 5

Their Lethes, their Styxes, and Stygians:
Their Quis, and their Quaes, and their Quods,
  They're all but a parcel of Pigeons.
        Toroddle, toroddle, toroll.

When Methodist preachers come down
  A-preaching that drinking is sinful,   10
I'll wager the rascals a crown
  They always preach best with a skinful.
But when you come down with your pence,
  For a slice of their scurvy religion,
I'll leave it to all men of sense,   15
  But you, my good friend, are the pigeon.
        Toroddle, toroddle, toroll.

Then come, put the jorum about,
  And let us be merry and clever;
Our hearts and our liquors are stout;
  Here's the Three Jolly Pigeons for ever.   20
Let some cry up woodcock or hare,
  Your bustards, your ducks, and your widgeons;
But of all the birds in the air,
  Here's a health to the Three Jolly Pigeons.
        Toroddle, toroddle, toroll.

EPILOGUE TO 'SHE STOOPS TO CONQUER'

WELL, having stoop'd to conquer with success,
And gain'd a husband without aid from dress,
Still, as a Bar-maid, I could wish it too,
As I have conquer'd him, to conquer you:
And let me say, for all your resolution,   5
That pretty Bar-maids have done execution.
Our life is all a play, compos'd to please,
'We have our exits and our entrances.'
The First Act shows the simple country maid,
Harmless and young, of ev'ry thing afraid;   10
Blushes when hir'd, and, with unmeaning action,
'I hopes as how to give you satisfaction.'
Her Second Act displays a livelier scene—
Th' unblushing Bar-maid of a country inn,
Who whisks about the house, at market caters,   15
Talks loud, coquets the guests, and scolds the waiters.
Next the scene shifts to town, and there she soars,
The chop-house toast of ogling connoisseurs.
On 'Squires and Cits she there displays her arts,
And on the gridiron broils her lovers' hearts: 20

And as she smiles, her triumphs to complete,
Even Common-Councilmen forget to eat.
The Fourth Act shows her wedded to the 'Squire,
And Madam now begins to hold it higher;
Pretends to taste, at Operas cries *caro*,   25
And quits her *Nancy Dawson*, for *Che faro*,
Doats upon dancing, and in all her pride,
Swims round the room, the Heinel of Cheapside;
Ogles and leers with artificial skill,
'Till having lost in age the power to kill,   30
She sits all night at cards, and ogles at spadille.
Such, through our lives, the eventful history—
The Fifth and Last Act still remains for me.
The Bar-maid now for your protection prays.
Turns Female Barrister, and pleads for Bayes.   35

RETALIATION A POEM

Of old, when Scarron his companions invited,
Each guest brought his dish, and the feast was united;
If our landlord supplies us with beef, and with fish,
Let each guest bring himself, and he brings the best dish:
Our Dean shall be venison, just fresh from the plains;   5
Our Burke shall be tongue, with a garnish of brains;
Our Will shall be wild-fowl, of excellent flavour,
And Dick with his pepper shall heighten their savour:
Our Cumberland's sweet-bread its place shall obtain,
And Douglas is pudding, substantial and plain: 10
Our Garrick's a salad; for in him we see
Oil, vinegar, sugar, and saltness agree:
To make out the dinner, full certain I am,
That Ridge is anchovy, and Reynolds is lamb;
That Hickey's a capon, and by the same rule,   15
Magnanimous Goldsmith a gooseberry fool.
At a dinner so various, at such a repast,
Who'd not be a glutton, and stick to the last?
Here, waiter! more wine, let me sit while I'm able,
Till all my companions sink under the table;   20
Then, with chaos and blunders encircling my head,
Let me ponder, and tell what I think of the dead.

  Here lies the good Dean, re-united to earth,
Who mix'd reason with pleasure, and wisdom with mirth:
If he had any faults, he has left us in doubt,   25
At least, in six weeks, I could not find 'em out;
Yet some have declar'd, and it can't be denied 'em,
That sly-boots was cursedly cunning to hide 'em.

   Here lies our good Edmund, whose genius was such,
We scarcely can praise it, or blame it too much;   30
Who, born for the Universe, narrow'd his mind,
And to party gave up what was meant for mankind.
Though fraught with all learning, yet straining his throat
To persuade Tommy Townshend to lend him a vote;
Who, too deep for his hearers, still went on refining,   35
And thought of convincing, while they thought of dining;
Though equal to all things, for all things unfit,
Too nice for a statesman, too proud for a wit:
For a patriot, too cool; for a drudge, disobedient;
And too fond of the *right* to pursue the *expedient*.   40
In short, 'twas his fate, unemploy'd, or in place, Sir,
To eat mutton cold, and cut blocks with a razor.

   Here lies honest William, whose heart was a mint,
While the owner ne'er knew half the good that was in't;
The pupil of impulse, it forc'd him along,   45
His conduct still right, with his argument wrong;
Still aiming at honour, yet fearing to roam,
The coachman was tipsy, the chariot drove home;
Would you ask for his merits? alas! he had none;
What was good was spontaneous, his faults were his own.   50

   Here lies honest Richard, whose fate I must sigh at;
Alas, that such frolic should now be so quiet!
What spirits were his! what wit and what whim!
Now breaking a jest, and now breaking a limb;
Now wrangling and grumbling to keep up the ball,   55
Now teasing and vexing, yet laughing at all!
In short, so provoking a devil was Dick,
That we wish'd him full ten times a day at Old Nick;
But, missing his mirth and agreeable vein,
As often we wish'd to have Dick back again.   60

   Here Cumberland lies, having acted his parts,
The Terence of England, the mender of hearts;
A flattering painter, who made it his care
To draw men as they ought to be, not as they are.
His gallants are all faultless, his women divine,   65
And comedy wonders at being so fine;
Like a tragedy queen he has dizen'd her out,
Or rather like tragedy giving a rout.
His fools have their follies so lost in a crowd
Of virtues and feelings, that folly grows proud;   70
And coxcombs, alike in their failings alone,
Adopting his portraits, are pleas'd with their own.

Say, where has our poet this malady caught?
Or, wherefore his characters thus without fault?
Say, was it that vainly directing his view   75
To find out men's virtues, and finding them few,
Quite sick of pursuing each troublesome elf,
He grew lazy at last, and drew from himself?

  Here Douglas retires, from his toils to relax,
The scourge of impostors, the terror of quacks: 80
Come, all ye quack bards, and ye quacking divines,
Come, and dance on the spot where your tyrant reclines:
When Satire and Censure encircl'd his throne,
I fear'd for your safety, I fear'd for my own;
But now he is gone, and we want a detector,   85
Our Dodds shall be pious, our Kenricks shall lecture;
Macpherson write bombast, and call it a style,
Our Townshend make speeches, and I shall compile;
New Lauders and Bowers the Tweed shall cross over,
No countryman living their tricks to discover;   90
Detection her taper shall quench to a spark,
And Scotchman meet Scotchman, and cheat in the dark.

  Here lies David Garrick, describe me, who can,
An abridgment of all that was pleasant in man;
As an actor, confess'd without rival to shine: 95
As a wit, if not first, in the very first line:
Yet, with talents like these, and an excellent heart,
The man had his failings, a dupe to his art.
Like an ill-judging beauty, his colours he spread,
And beplaster'd with rouge his own natural red.   100
On the stage he was natural, simple, affecting;
'Twas only that when he was off he was acting.
With no reason on earth to go out of his way,
He turn'd and he varied full ten times a day.
Though secure of our hearts, yet confoundedly sick 105
If they were not his own by finessing and trick,
He cast off his friends, as a huntsman his pack,
For he knew when he pleas'd he could whistle them back.
Of praise a mere glutton, he swallow'd what came,
And the puff of a dunce he mistook it for fame;   110
Till his relish grown callous, almost to disease,
Who pepper'd the highest was surest to please.
But let us be candid, and speak out our mind,
If dunces applauded, he paid them in kind.
Ye Kenricks, ye Kellys, and Woodfalls so grave,   115
What a commerce was yours, while you got and you gave!
How did Grub-street re-echo the shouts you rais'd,
While he was be-Roscius'd, and you were be-prais'd!

But peace to his spirit, wherever it flies,
To act as an angel, and mix with the skies: 120
Those poets, who owe their best fame to his skill,
Shall still be his flatterers, go where he will.
Old Shakespeare, receive him, with praise and with love,
And Beaumonts and Bens be his Kellys above.

  Here Hickey reclines, a most blunt, pleasant creature, 125
And slander itself must allow him good nature:
He cherish'd his friend, and he relish'd a bumper;
Yet one fault he had, and that one was a thumper.
Perhaps you may ask if the man was a miser!
I answer, no, no, for he always was wiser: 130
Too courteous, perhaps, or obligingly flat?
His very worst foe can't accuse him of that:
Perhaps he confided in men as they go,
And so was too foolishly honest! Ah no!
Then what was his failing? come, tell it, and burn ye! 135
He was, could he help it?—a special attorney.

  Here Reynolds is laid, and, to tell you my mind,
He has not left a better or wiser behind:
His pencil was striking, resistless, and grand;
His manners were gentle, complying, and bland;   140
Still born to improve us in every part,
His pencil our faces, his manners our heart:
To coxcombs averse, yet most civilly steering,
When they judg'd without skill he was still hard of hearing:
When they talk'd of their Raphaels, Correggios, and stuff, 145
He shifted his trumpet, and only took snuff.

POSTSCRIPT

After the Fourth Edition of this Poem was printed, the Publisher received an Epitaph on Mr. Whitefoord, from a friend of the late Doctor Goldsmith, inclosed in a letter, of which the following is an abstract:—

'I have in my possession a sheet of paper, containing near forty lines in the Doctor's own hand-writing: there are many scattered, broken verses, on Sir Jos. Reynolds, Counsellor Ridge, Mr. Beauclerk, and Mr. Whitefoord. The Epitaph on the last-mentioned gentleman is the only one that is finished, and therefore I have copied it, that you may add it to the next edition. It is a striking proof of Doctor Goldsmith's good-nature. I saw this sheet of paper in the Doctor's room, five or six days before he died; and, as I had got all the other Epitaphs, I asked him if I might take it. "*In truth you may, my Boy,*" (replied he,) "*for it will be of no use to me where I am going.*"

Here Whitefoord reclines, and deny it who can,
Though he *merrily* liv'd, he is now a 'grave' man;
Rare compound of oddity, frolic, and fun!
Who relish'd a joke, and rejoic'd in a pun;   150
Whose temper was generous, open, sincere;
A stranger to flatt'ry, a stranger to fear;
Who scatter'd around wit and humour at will;
Whose daily *bons mots* half a column might fill;
A Scotchman, from pride and from prejudice free;   155
A scholar, yet surely no pedant was he.

  What pity, alas! that so lib'ral a mind
Should so long be to news-paper essays confin'd;
Who perhaps to the summit of science could soar,
Yet content 'if the table he set on a roar';   160
Whose talents to fill any station were fit,
Yet happy if Woodfall confess'd him a wit.

  Ye news-paper witlings! ye pert scribbling folks
Who copied his squibs, and re-echoed his jokes;
Ye tame imitators, ye servile herd, come,   165
Still follow your master, and visit his tomb:
To deck it, bring with you festoons of the vine,
And copious libations bestow on his shrine:
Then strew all around it (you can do no less)
Cross-readings, Ship-news, and *Mistakes of the Press.*
                170

  Merry Whitefoord, farewell! for *thy* sake I admit
That a Scot may have humour, I had almost said wit:
This debt to thy mem'ry I cannot refuse,
'Thou best humour'd man with the worst humour'd muse.'

SONG
INTENDED TO HAVE BEEN SUNG IN 'SHE STOOPS TO CONQUER'

  Ah me! when shall I marry me?
    Lovers are plenty; but fail to relieve me:
  He, fond youth, that could carry me,
    Offers to love, but means to deceive me.

  But I will rally, and combat the ruiner: 5
    Not a look, not a smile shall my passion discover:
  She that gives all to the false one pursuing her,
    Makes but a penitent, loses a lover.

TRANSLATION ('CHASTE ARE THEIR INSTINCTS')

CHASTE are their instincts, faithful is their fire,
No foreign beauty tempts to false desire;
The snow-white vesture, and the glittering crown,
The simple plumage, or the glossy down
Prompt not their loves:—the patriot bird pursues   5
His well acquainted tints, and kindred hues.
Hence through their tribes no mix'd polluted flame,
No monster-breed to mark the groves with shame;
But the chaste blackbird, to its partner true,
Thinks black alone is beauty's favourite hue.   10
The nightingale, with mutual passion blest,
Sings to its mate, and nightly charms the nest;
While the dark owl to court its partner flies,
And owns its offspring in their yellow eyes.

THE HAUNCH OF VENISON
A POETICAL EPISTLE TO LORD CLARE

THANKS, my Lord, for your venison, for finer or fatter
Never rang'd in a forest, or smok'd in a platter;
The haunch was a picture for painters to study,
The fat was so white, and the lean was so ruddy.
Though my stomach was sharp, I could scarce help regretting   5
To spoil such a delicate picture by eating;
I had thoughts, in my chambers, to place it in view,
To be shown to my friends as a piece of *virtù*;
As in some Irish houses, where things are so so,
One gammon of bacon hangs up for a show: 10
But for eating a rasher of what they take pride in,
They'd as soon think of eating the pan it is fried in.
But hold—let me pause—Don't I hear you pronounce
This tale of the bacon a damnable bounce?
Well, suppose it a bounce—sure a poet may try,   15
By a bounce now and then, to get courage to fly.

  But, my Lord, it's no bounce: I protest in my turn,
It's a truth—and your Lordship may ask Mr. Byrne.
To go on with my tale—as I gaz'd on the haunch,
I thought of a friend that was trusty and staunch;   20
So I cut it, and sent it to Reynolds undress'd,
To paint it, or eat it, just as he lik'd best.
Of the neck and the breast I had next to dispose;
'Twas a neck and a breast—that might rival M—r—'s:
But in parting with these I was puzzled again,   25
With the how, and the who, and the where, and the when.

There's H—d, and C—y, and H—rth, and H—ff,
I think they love venison—I know they love beef;
There's my countryman H—gg—ns—Oh! let him alone,
For making a blunder, or picking a bone.   30
But hang it—to poets who seldom can eat,
Your very good mutton's a very good treat;
Such dainties to them, their health it might hurt,
It's like sending them ruffles, when wanting a shirt.
While thus I debated, in reverie centred,   35
An acquaintance, a friend as he call'd himself, enter'd;
An under-bred, fine-spoken fellow was he,
And he smil'd as he look'd at the venison and me.
'What have we got here?—Why, this is good eating!
Your own, I suppose—or is it in waiting?'   40
'Why, whose should it be?' cried I with a flounce,
'I get these things often;'—but that was a bounce:
'Some lords, my acquaintance, that settle the nation,
Are pleas'd to be kind—but I hate ostentation.'

'If that be the case, then,' cried he, very gay,   45
'I'm glad I have taken this house in my way.
To-morrow you take a poor dinner with me;
No words—I insist on't—precisely at three:
We'll have Johnson, and Burke; all the wits will be there;
My acquaintance is slight, or I'd ask my Lord Clare.   50
And now that I think on't, as I am a sinner!
We wanted this venison to make out the dinner.
What say you—a pasty? it shall, and it must,
And my wife, little Kitty, is famous for crust.
Here, porter!—this venison with me to Mile-end;   55
No stirring—I beg—my dear friend—my dear friend!
Thus snatching his hat, he brush'd off like the wind,
And the porter and eatables follow'd behind.

Left alone to reflect, having emptied my shelf,
'And nobody with me at sea but myself';   60
Though I could not help thinking my gentleman hasty,
Yet Johnson, and Burke, and a good venison pasty,
Were things that I never dislik'd in my life,
Though clogg'd with a coxcomb, and Kitty his wife.
So next day, in due splendour to make my approach,   65
I drove to his door in my own hackney coach.

When come to the place where we all were to dine,
(A chair-lumber'd closet just twelve feet by nine:)
My friend bade me welcome, but struck me quite dumb,
With tidings that Johnson and Burke would not come;   70

'For I knew it,' he cried, 'both eternally fail,
The one with his speeches, and t'other with Thrale;
But no matter, I'll warrant we'll make up the party
With two full as clever, and ten times as hearty.
The one is a Scotchman, the other a Jew,   75
They['re] both of them merry and authors like you;
The one writes the *Snarler*, the other the *Scourge*;
Some think he writes *Cinna*—he owns to *Panurge*.'
While thus he describ'd them by trade, and by name,
They enter'd and dinner was serv'd as they came.   80

  At the top a fried liver and bacon were seen,
At the bottom was tripe in a swinging tureen;
At the sides there was spinach and pudding made hot;
In the middle a place where the pasty—was not.
Now, my Lord as for tripe, it's my utter aversion,   85
And your bacon I hate like a Turk or a Persian;
So there I sat stuck, like a horse in a pound,
While the bacon and liver went merrily round.
But what vex'd me most was that d—'d Scottish rogue,
With his long-winded speeches, his smiles and his brogue; 90
And, 'Madam,' quoth he, 'may this bit be my poison,
A prettier dinner I never set eyes on;
Pray a slice of your liver, though may I be curs'd,
But I've eat of your tripe till I'm ready to burst.'
'The tripe,' quoth the Jew, with his chocolate cheek,   95
'I could dine on this tripe seven days in the week:
I like these here dinners so pretty and small;
But your friend there, the Doctor, eats nothing at all.'
'O—Oh!' quoth my friend, 'he'll come on in a trice,
He's keeping a corner for something that's nice: 100
There's a pasty'—'A pasty!' repeated the Jew,
'I don't care if I keep a corner for't too.'
'What the de'il, mon, a pasty!' re-echoed the Scot,
'Though splitting, I'll still keep a corner for thot.'
'We'll all keep a corner,' the lady cried out;   105
'We'll all keep a corner,' was echoed about.
While thus we resolv'd, and the pasty delay'd,
With look that quite petrified, enter'd the maid;
A visage so sad, and so pale with affright,
Wak'd Priam in drawing his curtains by night.   110
But we quickly found out, for who could mistake her?
That she came with some terrible news from the baker:
And so it fell out, for that negligent sloven
Had shut out the pasty on shutting his oven
Sad Philomel thus—but let similes drop—   115
And now that I think on't, the story may stop.
To be plain, my good Lord, it's but labour misplac'd

To send such good verses to one of your taste;
You've got an odd something—a kind of discerning—
A relish—a taste—sicken'd over by learning; 120
At least, it's your temper, as very well known,
That you think very slightly of all that's your own:
So, perhaps, in your habits of thinking amiss,
You may make a mistake, and think slightly of this.

EPITAPH ON THOMAS PARNELL

This tomb, inscrib'd to gentle Parnell's name,
May speak our gratitude, but not his fame.
What heart but feels his sweetly-moral lay,
That leads to truth through pleasure's flowery way!
Celestial themes confess'd his tuneful aid; 5
And Heaven, that lent him genius, was repaid.
Needless to him the tribute we bestow—
The transitory breath of fame below:
More lasting rapture from his works shall rise,
While Converts thank their poet in the skies. 10

THE CLOWN'S REPLY

John Trott was desired by two witty peers
To tell them the reason why asses had ears?
'An't please you,' quoth John, 'I'm not given to letters,
Nor dare I pretend to know more than my betters;
Howe'er, from this time I shall ne'er see your graces, 5
As I hope to be saved! without thinking on asses.'

EPITAPH ON EDWARD PURDON

Here lies poor Ned Purdon, from misery freed,
  Who long was a bookseller's hack;
He led such a damnable life in this world,—
  I don't think he'll wish to come back.

EPILOGUE FOR MR. LEE LEWES

Hold! Prompter, hold! a word before your nonsense;
I'd speak a word or two, to ease my conscience.
My pride forbids it ever should be said,
My heels eclips'd the honours of my head;
That I found humour in a piebald vest, 5
Or ever thought that jumping was a jest.

(*Takes off his mask.*)
Whence, and what art thou, visionary birth?
Nature disowns, and reason scorns thy mirth,
In thy black aspect every passion sleeps,
The joy that dimples, and the woe that weeps.   10
How has thou fill'd the scene with all thy brood,
Of fools pursuing, and of fools pursu'd!
Whose ins and outs no ray of sense discloses,
Whose only plot it is to break our noses;
Whilst from below the trap-door Demons rise,   15
And from above the dangling deities;
And shall I mix in this unhallow'd crew?
May rosined lightning blast me, if I do!
No—I will act, I'll vindicate the stage:
Shakespeare himself shall feel my tragic rage.   20
Off! off! vile trappings! a new passion reigns!
The madd'ning monarch revels in my veins.
Oh! for a Richard's voice to catch the theme:
'Give me another horse! bind up my wounds!—soft—
 'twas but a dream.'
Aye, 'twas but a dream, for now there's no retreating: 25
If I cease Harlequin, I cease from eating.
'Twas thus that Aesop's stag, a creature blameless,
Yet something vain, like one that shall be nameless,
Once on the margin of a fountain stood,
And cavill'd at his image in the flood.   30
'The deuce confound,' he cries, 'these drumstick shanks,
They never have my gratitude nor thanks;
They're perfectly disgraceful! strike me dead!
But for a head, yes, yes, I have a head.
How piercing is that eye! how sleek that brow!   35
My horns! I'm told horns are the fashion now.'
Whilst thus he spoke, astonish'd, to his view,
Near, and more near, the hounds and huntsmen drew.
'Hoicks! hark forward!' came thund'ring from behind,
He bounds aloft, outstrips the fleeting wind: 40
He quits the woods, and tries the beaten ways;
He starts, he pants, he takes the circling maze.
At length his silly head, so priz'd before,
Is taught his former folly to deplore;
Whilst his strong limbs conspire to set him free, 45
And at one bound he saves himself,—like me.
   (*Taking a jump through the stage door.*)

EPILOGUE
INTENDED TO HAVE BEEN SPOKEN FOR 'SHE STOOPS TO CONQUER' (1)

Enter MRS. BULKLEY, *who curtsies very low as beginning to speak. Then enter* MISS CATLEY, *who stands full before her, and curtsies to the audience.*

MRS. BULKLEY.
  HOLD, Ma'am, your pardon. What's your business here?

MISS CATLEY.
  The Epilogue.

MRS. BULKLEY.
     The Epilogue?

MISS CATLEY.
         Yes, the Epilogue, my dear.

MRS. BULKLEY.
  Sure you mistake, Ma'am. The Epilogue, *I* bring it.

MISS CATLEY.
  Excuse me, Ma'am. The Author bid *me* sing it.
Recitative.
  Ye beaux and belles, that form this splendid ring,   5
  Suspend your conversation while I sing.

MRS. BULKLEY.
  Why, sure the girl's beside herself: an Epilogue of singing,
  A hopeful end indeed to such a blest beginning.
  Besides, a singer in a comic set!—
  Excuse me, Ma'am, I know the etiquette.   10

MISS CATLEY.
  What if we leave it to the House?

MRS. BULKLEY.
     The House!—Agreed.

MISS CATLEY.
         Agreed.

MRS. BULKLEY.
  And she, whose party's largest, shall proceed.
  And first I hope, you'll readily agree
  I've all the critics and the wits for me.
  They, I am sure, will answer my commands: 15
  Ye candid-judging few, hold up your hands.
  What! no return? I find too late, I fear,
  That modern judges seldom enter here.

MISS CATLEY.
   I'm for a different set.—Old men, whose trade is
   Still to gallant and dangle with the ladies;—   20
Recitative.
   Who mump their passion, and who, grimly smiling,
   Still thus address the fair with voice beguiling:—
Air—Cotillon.
     Turn, my fairest, turn, if ever
      Strephon caught thy ravish'd eye;
     Pity take on your swain so clever,   25
      Who without your aid must die.
         Yes, I shall die, hu, hu, hu, hu!
         Yes, I must die, ho, ho, ho, ho!
          (*Da capo.*)

MRS. BULKLEY.
   Let all the old pay homage to your merit;
   Give me the young, the gay, the men of spirit.   30
   Ye travell'd tribe, ye macaroni train,
   Of French friseurs, and nosegays, justly vain,
   Who take a trip to Paris once a year
   To dress, and look like awkward Frenchmen here,
   Lend me your hands.—Oh! fatal news to tell: 35
   Their hands are only lent to the Heinel.

MISS CATLEY.
   Ay, take your travellers, travellers indeed!
   Give me my bonny Scot, that travels from the Tweed.
   Where are the chiels? Ah! Ah, I well discern
   The smiling looks of each bewitching bairn.   40
Air—A bonny young lad is my Jockey.
   I'll sing to amuse you by night and by day,
   And be unco merry when you are but gay;
   When you with your bagpipes are ready to play,
   My voice shall be ready to carol away
     With Sandy, and Sawney, and Jockey   45
     With Sawney, and Jarvie, and Jockey.

MRS. BULKLEY.
   Ye gamesters, who, so eager in pursuit,
   Make but of all your fortune one *va toute*;
   Ye jockey tribe, whose stock of words are few,
   'I hold the odds.—Done, done, with you, with you;'   50
   Ye barristers, so fluent with grimace,
   'My Lord,—your Lordship misconceives the case;'
   Doctors, who cough and answer every misfortuner,
   'I wish I'd been called in a little sooner:'
   Assist my cause with hands and voices hearty;   55

    Come, end the contest here, and aid my party.

MISS CATLEY.
Air—Ballinamony.
    Ye brave Irish lads, hark away to the crack,
    Assist me, I pray, in this woful attack;
    For sure I don't wrong you, you seldom are slack,
    When the ladies are calling, to blush and hang back; 60
      For you're always polite and attentive,
      Still to amuse us inventive,
      And death is your only preventive:
        Your hands and your voices for me.

MRS. BULKLEY.
    Well, Madam, what if, after all this sparring,   65
    We both agree, like friends, to end our jarring?

MISS CATLEY.
    And that our friendship may remain unbroken,
    What if we leave the Epilogue unspoken?

MRS. BULKLEY.
    Agreed.

MISS CATLEY.
    Agreed.

MRS. BULKLEY.
      And now with late repentance,
    Un-epilogued the Poet waits his sentence.   70
    Condemn the stubborn fool who can't submit
    To thrive by flattery, though he starves by wit.
        (*Exeunt.*)

EPILOGUE
INTENDED TO HAVE BEEN SPOKEN FOR 'SHE STOOPS TO CONQUER' (2)

T<small>HERE</small> is a place, so Ariosto sings,
A treasury for lost and missing things;
Lost human wits have places assign'd them,
And they, who lose their senses, there may find them.
But where's this place, this storehouse of the age?   5
The Moon, says he:—but *I* affirm the Stage:
At least in many things, I think, I see
His lunar, and our mimic world agree.
Both shine at night, for, but at Foote's alone,
We scarce exhibit till the sun goes down.   10

Both prone to change, no settled limits fix,
And sure the folks of both are lunatics.
But in this parallel my best pretence is,
That mortals visit both to find their senses.
To this strange spot, Rakes, Macaronies, Cits   15
Come thronging to collect their scatter'd wits.
The gay coquette, who ogles all the day,
Comes here at night, and goes a prude away.
Hither the affected city dame advancing,
Who sighs for operas, and dotes on dancing,   20
Taught by our art her ridicule to pause on,
Quits the *Ballet*, and calls for *Nancy Dawson*.
The Gamester too, whose wit's all high or low,
Oft risks his fortune on one desperate throw,
Comes here to saunter, having made his bets,   25
Finds his lost senses out, and pay his debts.
The Mohawk too—with angry phrases stored,
As 'D— —, Sir,' and 'Sir, I wear a sword';
Here lesson'd for a while, and hence retreating,
Goes out, affronts his man, and takes a beating.   30
Here come the sons of scandal and of news,
But find no sense—for they had none to lose.
Of all the tribe here wanting an adviser
Our Author's the least likely to grow wiser;
Has he not seen how you your favour place,   35
On sentimental Queens and Lords in lace?
Without a star, a coronet or garter,
How can the piece expect or hope for quarter?
No high-life scenes, no sentiment:—the creature
Still stoops among the low to copy nature.   40
Yes, he's far gone:—and yet some pity fix,
The English laws forbid to punish lunatics.

THE CAPTIVITY: AN ORATORIO

THE PERSONS.

FIRST ISRAELITISH PROPHET.
SECOND ISRAELITISH PROPHET.
ISRAELITISH WOMAN.
FIRST CHALDEAN PRIEST.
SECOND CHALDEAN PRIEST.
CHALDEAN WOMAN.
CHORUS OF YOUTHS AND VIRGINS.

Scene—The Banks of the River Euphrates, near Babylon.

THE CAPTIVITY

ACT I

SCENE I.
Israelites sitting on the Banks of the Euphrates.

FIRST PROPHET.

RECITATIVE.

Ye captive tribes, that hourly work and weep
Where flows Euphrates murmuring to the deep,
Suspend awhile the task, the tear suspend,
And turn to God, your Father and your Friend.
Insulted, chain'd, and all the world a foe,   5
Our God alone is all we boast below.

FIRST PROPHET.
AIR.
    Our God is all we boast below,
      To him we turn our eyes;
    And every added weight of woe
      Shall make our homage rise.   10

SECOND PROPHET.
    And though no temple richly drest,
      Nor sacrifice is here;
    We'll make his temple in our breast,
      And offer up a tear.
    [*The first stanza repeated by the Chorus.*

SECOND PROPHET.
RECITATIVE.
    That strain once more; it bids remembrance rise,   15
    And brings my long-lost country to mine eyes.
    Ye fields of Sharon, dress'd in flow'ry pride,
    Ye plains where Jordan rolls its glassy tide,
    Ye hills of Lebanon, with cedars crown'd,
    Ye Gilead groves, that fling perfumes around,   20
    These hills how sweet! Those plains how wond'rous fair,
    But sweeter still, when Heaven was with us there!

AIR.
    O Memory, thou fond deceiver,
      Still importunate and vain;

    To former joys recurring ever,   25
      And turning all the past to pain;

    Hence intruder, most distressing,
      Seek the happy and the free:
    The wretch who wants each other blessing,
      Ever wants a friend in thee.   30

FIRST PROPHET.
RECITATIVE.
  Yet, why complain? What, though by bonds confin'd,
  Should bonds repress the vigour of the mind?
  Have we not cause for triumph when we see
  Ourselves alone from idol-worship free?
  Are not this very morn those feasts begun?   35
  Where prostrate error hails the rising sun?
  Do not our tyrant lords this day ordain
  For superstitious rites and mirth profane?
  And should we mourn? Should coward virtue fly,
  When impious folly rears her front on high?   40
  No; rather let us triumph still the more,
  And as our fortune sinks, our wishes soar.

AIR.
    The triumphs that on vice attend
    Shall ever in confusion end;
    The good man suffers but to gain,   45
    And every virtue springs from pain:

    As aromatic plants bestow
    No spicy fragrance while they grow;
    But crush'd, or trodden to the ground,
    Diffuse their balmy sweets around.   50

SECOND PROPHET.
RECITATIVE.
  But hush, my sons, our tyrant lords are near;
  The sounds of barb'rous pleasure strike mine ear;
  Triumphant music floats along the vale;
  Near, nearer still, it gathers on the gale;
  The growing sound their swift approach declares;—   55
  Desist, my sons, nor mix the strain with theirs.

Enter CHALDEAN PRIESTS *attended.*
FIRST PRIEST.
AIR.
  Come on, my companions, the triumph display;
    Let rapture the minutes employ;
  The sun calls us out on this festival day,

    And our monarch partakes in the joy.   60

SECOND PRIEST.
  Like the sun, our great monarch all rapture supplies,
    Both similar blessings bestow;
  The sun with his splendour illumines the skies,
    And our monarch enlivens below.

A CHALDEAN WOMAN.
AIR.
  Haste, ye sprightly sons of pleasure;   65
  Love presents the fairest treasure,
    Leave all other joys for me.

A CHALDEAN ATTENDANT.
  Or rather, Love's delights despising,
  Haste to raptures ever rising
    Wine shall bless the brave and free.   70

FIRST PRIEST.
  Wine and beauty thus inviting,
  Each to different joys exciting,
    Whither shall my choice incline?

SECOND PRIEST.
  I'll waste no longer thought in choosing;
  But, neither this nor that refusing,   75
    I'll make them both together mine.

RECITATIVE.
  But whence, when joy should brighten o'er the land,
  This sullen gloom in Judah's captive band?
  Ye sons of Judah, why the lute unstrung?
  Or why those harps on yonder willows hung?   80
  Come, take the lyre, and pour the strain along,
  The day demands it; sing us Sion's song.
  Dismiss your griefs, and join our warbling choir,
  For who like you can wake the sleeping lyre?

SECOND PROPHET.
  Bow'd down with chains, the scorn of all mankind,   85
  To want, to toil, and every ill consign'd,
  Is this a time to bid us raise the strain,
  Or mix in rites that Heaven regards with pain?
  No, never! May this hand forget each art
  That speeds the power of music to the heart,   90
  Ere I forget the land that gave me birth,
  Or join with sounds profane its sacred mirth!

FIRST PRIEST.

   Insulting slaves! If gentler methods fail,
   The whips and angry tortures shall prevail.

      [*Exeunt Chaldeans*
FIRST PROPHET.
   Why, let them come, one good remains to cheer;   95
   We fear the Lord, and know no other fear.

CHORUS.
   Can whips or tortures hurt the mind
   On God's supporting breast reclin'd?
   Stand fast, and let our tyrants see
   That fortitude is victory.
         [*Exeunt.*

ACT II.

Scene as before. CHORUS OF ISRAELITES.
    O PEACE of mind, angelic guest!
    Thou soft companion of the breast!
     Dispense thy balmy store.
    Wing all our thoughts to reach the skies,
    Till earth, receding from our eyes,   5
     Shall vanish as we soar.

FIRST PRIEST.
RECITATIVE.
   No more! Too long has justice been delay'd,
   The king's commands must fully be obey'd;
   Compliance with his will your peace secures,
   Praise but our gods, and every good is yours.   10
   But if, rebellious to his high command,
   You spurn the favours offer'd from his hand,
   Think, timely think, what terrors are behind;
   Reflect, nor tempt to rage the royal mind.

SECOND PRIEST.
AIR.
     Fierce is the whirlwind howling   15
      O'er Afric's sandy plain,
     And fierce the tempest rolling
      Along the furrow'd main:
       But storms that fly,
       To rend the sky,   20
      Every ill presaging,
       Less dreadful show
       To worlds below
      Than angry monarch's raging.

ISRAELITISH WOMAN.
RECITATIVE.
    Ah, me! What angry terrors round us grow;   25
    How shrinks my soul to meet the threaten'd blow!
    Ye prophets, skill'd in Heaven's eternal truth,
    Forgive my sex's fears, forgive my youth!
    If, shrinking thus, when frowning power appears,
    I wish for life, and yield me to my fears.   30
    Let us one hour, one little hour obey;
    To-morrow's tears may wash our stains away.

AIR.
    To the last moment of his breath
      On hope the wretch relies;
    And e'en the pang preceding death   35
      Bids expectation rise.

    Hope, like the gleaming taper's light,
      Adorns and cheers our way;
    And still, as darker grows the night,
      Emits a brighter ray.   40

SECOND PRIEST. RECITATIVE.
    Why this delay? At length for joy prepare;
    I read your looks, and see compliance there.
    Come on, and bid the warbling rapture rise,
    Our monarch's fame the noblest theme supplies.
    Begin, ye captive bands, and strike the lyre,   45
    The time, the theme, the place, and all conspire.

CHALDEAN WOMAN.
AIR.
    See the ruddy morning smiling,
    Hear the grove to bliss beguiling;
    Zephyrs through the woodland playing,
    Streams along the valley straying.   50

FIRST PRIEST.
    While these a constant revel keep,
    Shall Reason only teach to weep?
    Hence, intruder! We'll pursue
    Nature, a better guide than you.

SECOND PRIEST.
    Every moment, as it flows,   55
    Some peculiar pleasure owes;
    Then let us, providently wise,
    Seize the debtor as it flies.

    Think not to-morrow can repay
    The pleasures that we lose to-day;   60
    To-morrow's most unbounded store
    Can but pay its proper score.

FIRST PRIEST.
RECITATIVE.
  But hush! See, foremost of the captive choir,
  The master-prophet grasps his full-ton'd lyre.
  Mark where he sits, with executing art,   65
  Feels for each tone, and speeds it to the heart;
  See how prophetic rapture fills his form,
  Awful as clouds that nurse the growing storm;
  And now his voice, accordant to the string,
  Prepares our monarch's victories to sing.   70

FIRST PROPHET.
AIR.
    From north, from south, from east, from west,
      Conspiring nations come;
    Tremble thou vice-polluted breast;
      Blasphemers, all be dumb.

    The tempest gathers all around,   75
      On Babylon it lies;
    Down with her! down—down to the ground;
      She sinks, she groans, she dies.

SECOND PROPHET.
    Down with her, Lord, to lick the dust,
      Ere yonder setting sun;   80
    Serve her as she hath served the just!
      'Tis fixed—it shall be done.

FIRST PRIEST.
RECITATIVE.
  No more! When slaves thus insolent presume,
  The king himself shall judge, and fix their doom.
  Unthinking wretches! have not you, and all,   85
  Beheld our power in Zedekiah's fall?
  To yonder gloomy dungeon turn your eyes;
  See where dethron'd your captive monarch lies,
  Depriv'd of sight and rankling in his chain;
  See where he mourns his friends and children slain.   90
  Yet know, ye slaves, that still remain behind
  More ponderous chains, and dungeons more confin'd.

CHORUS OF ALL.

Arise, all potent ruler, rise,
     And vindicate thy people's cause;
   Till every tongue in every land   95
     Shall offer up unfeign'd applause.
          [*Exeunt.*

ACT III.

Scene as before.

FIRST PRIEST.
RECITATIVE.
  YES, my companions, Heaven's decrees are past,
  And our fix'd empire shall for ever last;
  In vain the madd'ning prophet threatens woe,
  In vain rebellion aims her secret blow;
  Still shall our fame and growing power be spread,   5
  And still our vengeance crush the traitor's head.

AIR.
      Coeval with man
      Our empire began,
      And never shall fail
      Till ruin shakes all;   10
      When ruin shakes all,
      Then shall Babylon fall.

FIRST PROPHET.
RECITATIVE.
  'Tis thus that pride triumphant rears the head,
  A little while, and all their power is fled;
  But ha! what means yon sadly plaintive train,   15
  That this way slowly bend along the plain?
  And now, methinks, to yonder bank they bear
  A palled corse, and rest the body there.
  Alas! too well mine eyes indignant trace
  The last remains of Judah's royal race: 20
  Our monarch falls, and now our fears are o'er,
  Unhappy Zedekiah is no more!

AIR.
      Ye wretches who, by fortune's hate,
        In want and sorrow groan;
      Come ponder his severer fate,   25
        And learn to bless your own.

      You vain, whom youth and pleasure guide,
        Awhile the bliss suspend;
      Like yours, his life began in pride,

    Like his, your lives shall end.   30

SECOND PROPHET.
RECITATIVE.
  Behold his wretched corse with sorrow worn,
  His squalid limbs with pond'rous fetters torn;
  Those eyeless orbs that shock with ghastly glare,
  Those ill-becoming rags—that matted hair!
  And shall not Heaven for this its terrors show,   35
  Grasp the red bolt, and lay the guilty low?
  How long, how long, Almighty God of all,
  Shall wrath vindictive threaten ere it fall!

ISRAELITISH WOMAN.
AIR.
    As panting flies the hunted hind,
      Where brooks refreshing stray;   40
    And rivers through the valley wind,
      That stop the hunter's way:

    Thus we, O Lord, alike distrest,
      For streams of mercy long;
    Those streams which cheer the sore opprest,   45
      And overwhelm the strong.

FIRST PROPHET.
RECITATIVE.
  But, whence that shout? Good heavens! amazement all!
  See yonder tower just nodding to the fall:
  See where an army covers all the ground,
  Saps the strong wall, and pours destruction round;   50
  The ruin smokes, destruction pours along;
  How low the great, how feeble are the strong!
  The foe prevails, the lofty walls recline—
  O God of hosts, the victory is thine!

CHORUS OF ISRAELITES.
    Down with them, Lord, to lick the dust;   55
      Thy vengeance be begun:
    Serve them as they have serv'd the just,
      And let thy will be done.

FIRST PRIEST.
RECITATIVE.
  All, all is lost. The Syrian army fails,
  Cyrus, the conqueror of the world, prevails,   60
  The ruin smokes, the torrent pours along;
  How low the proud, how feeble are the strong!
  Save us, O Lord! to thee, though late, we pray,

And give repentance but an hour's delay.

FIRST AND SECOND PRIEST.
AIR.
    Thrice happy, who in happy hour   65
      To Heaven their praise bestow,
    And own his all-consuming power
      Before they feel the blow!

FIRST PROPHET.
RECITATIVE.
  Now, now's our time! ye wretches bold and blind,
  Brave but to God, and cowards to mankind,   70
  Too late you seek that power unsought before,
  Your wealth, your pride, your kingdom, are no more.

AIR.
    O Lucifer, thou son of morn,
      Alike of Heaven and man the foe;
      Heaven, men, and all,   75
      Now press thy fall,
    And sink thee lowest of the low.

FIRST PROPHET.
    O Babylon, how art thou fallen!
      Thy fall more dreadful from delay!
      Thy streets forlorn   80
      To wilds shall turn,
    Where toads shall pant, and vultures prey.

SECOND PROPHET.
RECITATIVE.
  Such be her fate. But listen! from afar
  The clarion's note proclaims the finish'd war!
  Cyrus, our great restorer, is at hand,   85
  And this way leads his formidable band.
  Give, give your songs of Sion to the wind,
  And hail the benefactor of mankind:
  He comes pursuant to divine decree,
  To chain the strong, and set the captive free.   90

CHORUS OF YOUTHS.
    Rise to transports past expressing,
      Sweeter from remember'd woes;
    Cyrus comes, our wrongs redressing,
      Comes to give the world repose.

CHORUS OF VIRGINS.
    Cyrus comes, the world redressing,   95
      Love and pleasure in his train;

    Comes to heighten every blessing,
      Comes to soften every pain.

SEMI-CHORUS.
    Hail to him with mercy reigning,
      Skilled in every peaceful art;   100
    Who from bonds our limbs unchaining,
      Only binds the willing heart.

THE LAST CHORUS.
  But chief to Thee, our God, defender, friend,
    Let praise be given to all eternity;
  O Thou, without beginning, without end,   105
    Let us, and all, begin and end, in Thee!

VERSES IN REPLY TO AN INVITATION TO DINNER AT DR. BAKER'S.

'This is *a poem! This* is *a copy of verses!'*

Your mandate I got,
You may all go to pot;
Had your senses been right,
You'd have sent before night;
As I hope to be saved,   5
I put off being shaved;
For I could not make bold,
While the matter was cold,
To meddle in suds,
Or to put on my duds;   10
So tell Horneck and Nesbitt,
And Baker and his bit,
And Kauffmann beside,
And the Jessamy Bride,
With the rest of the crew,   15
The Reynoldses two,
Little Comedy's face,
And the Captain in lace,
(By-the-bye you may tell him,
I have something to sell him;   20
Of use I insist,
When he comes to enlist.
Your worships must know
That a few days ago,
An order went out,   25
For the foot guards so stout
To wear tails in high taste,
Twelve inches at least:

                    Now I've got him a scale
                    To measure each tail,   30
                    To lengthen a short tail,
                    And a long one to curtail.)—
                      Yet how can I when vext,
                    Thus stray from my text?
                    Tell each other to rue   35
                    Your Devonshire crew,
                    For sending so late
                    To one of my state.
                    But 'tis Reynolds's way
                    From wisdom to stray,   40
                    And Angelica's whim
                    To be frolick like him,
But, alas! Your good worships, how could they be wiser,
When both have been spoil'd in to-day's *Advertiser*?
OLIVER GOLDSMITH.

LETTER IN PROSE AND VERSE TO MRS. BUNBURY

Madam,
I read your letter with all that allowance which critical candour could require, but after all find so much to object to, and so much to raise my indignation, that I cannot help giving it a serious answer.

I am not so ignorant, Madam, as not to see there are many sarcasms contained in it, and solecisms also. (Solecism is a word that comes from the town of Soleis in Attica, among the Greeks, built by Solon, and applied as we use the word Kidderminster for curtains, from a town also of that name;—but this is learning you have no taste for!)—I say, Madam, there are sarcasms in it, and solecisms also. But not to seem an ill-natured critic, I'll take leave to quote your own words, and give you my remarks upon them as they occur. You begin as follows:—

> 'I hope, my good Doctor, you soon will be here,
> And your spring-velvet coat very smart will appear,
> To open our ball the first day of the year.'

Pray, Madam, where did you ever find the epithet 'good,' applied to the title of Doctor? Had you called me 'learned Doctor,' or 'grave Doctor,' or 'noble Doctor,' it might be allowable, because they belong to the profession. But, not to cavil at trifles, you talk of my 'spring-velvet coat,' and advise me to wear it the first day in the year,—that is, in the middle of winter!—a spring-velvet in the middle of winter!!! That would be a solecism indeed! and yet, to increase the inconsistence, in another part of your letter you call me a beau. Now, on one side or other, you must be wrong. If I am a beau, I can never think of wearing a spring-velvet in winter: and if I am not a beau, why then, that explains itself. But let me go on to your two next strange lines:—

> 'And bring with you a wig, that is modish and gay,
> dance with the girls that are makers of hay.'

The absurdity of making hay at Christmas, you yourself seem sensible of: you say your sister will laugh; and so indeed she well may! The Latins have an expression for a contemptuous sort of laughter, 'Naso contemnere adunco'; that is, to laugh with a crooked nose. She may laugh at you in the manner of the ancients if she thinks fit. But now I come to the most extraordinary of all extraordinary propositions, which is, to take your and your sister's advice in playing at loo. The presumption of the offer raises my indignation beyond the bounds of prose; it inspires me at once with verse and resentment. I take advice! and from whom? You shall hear.

First let me suppose, what may shortly be true,
The company set, and the word to be, Loo;
All smirking, and pleasant, and big with adventure,
And ogling the stake which is fix'd in the centre.
Round and round go the cards, while I inwardly damn   5
At never once finding a visit from Pam.
I lay down my stake, apparently cool,
While the harpies about me all pocket the pool.
I fret in my gizzard, yet, cautious and sly,
I wish all my friends may be bolder than I: 10
Yet still they sit snug, not a creature will aim
By losing their money to venture at fame.
'Tis in vain that at niggardly caution I scold,
'Tis in vain that I flatter the brave and the bold:
All play their own way, and they think me an ass,—   15
'What does Mrs. Bunbury?' 'I, Sir? I pass.'
'Pray what does Miss Horneck? Take courage, come do,'—
'Who, I? let me see, Sir, why I must pass too.'
Mr. Bunbury frets, and I fret like the devil,
To see them so cowardly, lucky, and civil.   20
Yet still I sit snug, and continue to sigh on,
Till made by my losses as bold as a lion,
I venture at all,—while my avarice regards
The whole pool as my own—'Come, give me five cards.'
'Well done!' cry the ladies; 'Ah, Doctor, that's good!   25
The pool's very rich—ah! the Doctor is loo'd!'
Thus foil'd in my courage, on all sides perplex'd,
I ask for advice from the lady that's next:
'Pray, Ma'am, be so good as to give your advice;
Don't you think the best way is to venture for 't twice?' 30
'I advise,' cries the lady, 'to try it, I own.—
Ah! the Doctor is loo'd! Come, Doctor, put down.'

Thus, playing, and playing, I still grow more eager,
And so bold, and so bold, I'm at last a bold beggar.
Now, ladies, I ask, if law-matters you're skill'd in,   35
Whether crimes such as yours should not come before Fielding?
For giving advice that is not worth a straw,
May well be call'd picking of pockets in law;
And picking of pockets, with which I now charge ye,
Is, by quinto Elizabeth, Death without Clergy.   40
What justice, when both to the Old Bailey brought!
By the gods, I'll enjoy it; though 'tis but in thought!
Both are plac'd at the bar, with all proper decorum,
With bunches of fennel, and nosegays before 'em;
Both cover their faces with mobs and all that;   45
But the judge bids them, angrily, take off their hat.
When uncover'd, a buzz of enquiry runs round,—
'Pray what are their crimes?'—'They've been pilfering found.'
'But, pray, whom have they pilfer'd?'—'A Doctor, I hear.'
'What, yon solemn-faced, odd-looking man that stands near!'   50
'The same.'—'What a pity! how does it surprise one!
Two handsomer culprits I never set eyes on!'
Then their friends all come round me with cringing and leering,
To melt me to pity, and soften my swearing.
First Sir Charles advances with phrases well strung,   55
'Consider, dear Doctor, the girls are but young.'
'The younger the worse,' I return him again,
'It shows that their habits are all dyed in grain.'
'But then they're so handsome, one's bosom it grieves.'
'What signifies *handsome*, when people are thieves?'   60
'But where is your justice? their cases are hard.'
'What signifies *justice*? I want the *reward*.

There's the parish of Edmonton offers forty pounds; there's the parish of St. Leonard, Shoreditch, offers forty pounds; there's the parish of Tyburn, from the Hog-in-the-Pound to St. Giles's watchhouse, offers forty pounds,—I shall have all that if I convict them!'—

'But consider their case,—it may yet be your own!
And see how they kneel! Is your heart made of stone?'
This moves:—so at last I agree to relent,   65
For ten pounds in hand, and ten pounds to be spent.

I challenge you all to answer this: I tell you, you cannot. It cuts deep;—but now for the rest of the letter: and next— but I want room—so I believe I shall battle the rest out at Barton some day next week.

I don't value you all!
O. G.

VIDA'S GAME OF CHESS
TRANSLATED

Armies of box that sportively engage
And mimic real battles in their rage,
Pleased I recount; how, smit with glory's charms,
Two mighty Monarchs met in adverse arms,
Sable and white; assist me to explore,   5
Ye Serian Nymphs, what ne'er was sung before.
No path appears: yet resolute I stray
Where youth undaunted bids me force my way.
O'er rocks and cliffs while I the task pursue,
Guide me, ye Nymphs, with your unerring clue.   10
For you the rise of this diversion know,
You first were pleased in Italy to show
This studious sport; from Scacchis was its name,
The pleasing record of your Sister's fame.
  When Jove through Ethiopia's parch'd extent   15
To grace the nuptials of old Ocean went,
Each god was there; and mirth and joy around
To shores remote diffused their happy sound.
Then when their hunger and their thirst no more
Claim'd their attention, and the feast was o'er;   20
Ocean with pastime to divert the thought,
Commands a painted table to be brought.
Sixty-four spaces fill the chequer'd square;
Eight in each rank eight equal limits share.
Alike their form, but different are their dyes,   25
They fade alternate, and alternate rise,
White after black; such various stains as those
The shelving backs of tortoises disclose.
Then to the gods that mute and wondering sate,
You see (says he) the field prepared for fate.   30
Here will the little armies please your sight,
With adverse colours hurrying to the fight:
On which so oft, with silent sweet surprise,
The Nymphs and Nereids used to feast their eyes,
And all the neighbours of the hoary deep,   35
When calm the sea, and winds were lull'd asleep
But see, the mimic heroes tread the board;
He said, and straightway from an urn he pour'd
The sculptured box, that neatly seem'd to ape
The graceful figure of a human shape:—   40
Equal the strength and number of each foe,
Sixteen appear'd like jet, sixteen like snow.
As their shape varies various is the name,
Different their posts, nor is their strength the same.
There might you see two Kings with equal pride   45

Gird on their arms, their Consorts by their side;
Here the Foot-warriors glowing after fame,
There prancing Knights and dexterous Archers came
And Elephants, that on their backs sustain
Vast towers of war, and fill and shake the plain.   50
  And now both hosts, preparing for the storm
Of adverse battle, their encampments form.
In the fourth space, and on the farthest line,
Directly opposite the Monarchs shine;
The swarthy on white ground, on sable stands   55
The silver King; and then they send commands.
Nearest to these the Queens exert their might;
One the left side, and t'other guards the right:
Where each, by her respective armour known.
Chooses the colour that is like her own.   60
Then the young Archers, two that snowy-white
Bend the tough yew, and two as black as night;
(Greece call'd them Mars's favourites heretofore,
From their delight in war, and thirst of gore).
These on each side the Monarch and his Queen   65
Surround obedient; next to these are seen
The crested Knights in golden armour gay;
Their steeds by turns curvet, or snort or neigh.
In either army on each distant wing
Two mighty Elephants their castles bring,   70
Bulwarks immense! and then at last combine
Eight of the Foot to form the second line,
The vanguard to the King and Queen; from far
Prepared to open all the fate of war.
So moved the boxen hosts, each double-lined,   75
Their different colours floating in the wind:
As if an army of the Gauls should go,
With their white standards, o'er the Alpine snow
To meet in rigid fight on scorching sands
The sun-burnt Moors and Memnon's swarthy bands.   80
  Then Father Ocean thus; you see them here,
Celestial powers, what troops, what camps appear.
Learn now the sev'ral orders of the fray,
For e'en these arms their stated laws obey.
To lead the fight, the Kings from all their bands   85
Choose whom they please to bear their great commands.
Should a black hero first to battle go,
Instant a white one guards against the blow;
But only one at once can charge or shun the foe.
Their gen'ral purpose on one scheme is bent,   90
So to besiege the King within the tent,
That there remains no place by subtle flight
From danger free; and that decides the fight.

Meanwhile, howe'er, the sooner to destroy
Th' imperial Prince, remorseless they employ 95
Their swords in blood; and whosoever dare
Oppose their vengeance, in the ruin share.
Fate thins their camp; the parti-coloured field
Widens apace, as they o'ercome or yield,
But the proud victor takes the captive's post; 100
There fronts the fury of th' avenging host
One single shock: and (should he ward the blow),
May then retire at pleasure from the foe.
The Foot alone (so their harsh laws ordain)
When they proceed can ne'er return again. 105
 But neither all rush on alike to prove
The terror of their arms: The Foot must move
Directly on, and but a single square;
Yet may these heroes, when they first prepare
To mix in combat on the bloody mead, 110
Double their sally, and two steps proceed;
But when they wound, their swords they subtly guide
With aim oblique, and slanting pierce his side.
But the great Indian beasts, whose backs sustain
Vast turrets arm'd, when on the redd'ning plain 115
They join in all the terror of the fight,
Forward or backward, to the left or right,
Run furious, and impatient of confine
Scour through the field, and threat the farthest line.
Yet must they ne'er obliquely aim their blows; 120
That only manner is allow'd to those
Whom Mars has favour'd most, who bend the stubborn bows.
These glancing sidewards in a straight career,
Yet each confin'd to their respective sphere,
Or white or black, can send th' unerring dart 125
Wing'd with swift death to pierce through ev'ry part.
The fiery steed, regardless of the reins,
Comes prancing on; but sullenly disdains
The path direct, and boldly wheeling round,
Leaps o'er a double space at ev'ry bound: 130
And shifts from white or black to diff'rent colour'd ground.
But the fierce Queen, whom dangers ne'er dismay,
The strength and terror of the bloody day,
In a straight line spreads her destruction wide,
To left or right, before, behind, aside. 135
Yet may she never with a circling course
Sweep to the battle like the fretful Horse;
But unconfin'd may at her pleasure stray,
If neither friend nor foe block up the way;
For to o'erleap a warrior, 'tis decreed 140
Those only dare who curb the snorting steed.

With greater caution and majestic state
The warlike Monarchs in the scene of fate
Direct their motions, since for these appear
Zealous each hope, and anxious ev'ry fear.   145
While the King's safe, with resolution stern
They clasp their arms; but should a sudden turn
Make him a captive, instantly they yield,
Resolved to share his fortune in the field.
He moves on slow; with reverence profound   150
His faithful troops encompass him around,
And oft, to break some instant fatal scheme,
Rush to their fates, their sov'reign to redeem;
While he, unanxious where to wound the foe,
Need only shift and guard against a blow.   155
But none, however, can presume t' appear
Within his reach, but must his vengeance fear;
For he on ev'ry side his terror throws;
But when he changes from his first repose,
Moves but one step, most awfully sedate,   160
Or idly roving, or intent on fate.
These are the sev'ral and establish'd laws:
Now see how each maintains his bloody cause.
  Here paused the god, but (since whene'er they wage
War here on earth the gods themselves engage   165
In mutual battle as they hate or love,
And the most stubborn war is oft above),
Almighty Jove commands the circling train
Of gods from fav'ring either to abstain,
And let the fight be silently survey'd;   170
And added solemn threats if disobey'd.
Then call'd he Phoebus from among the Powers
And subtle Hermes, whom in softer hours
Fair Maia bore: youth wanton'd in their face;
Both in life's bloom, both shone with equal grace.   175
Hermes as yet had never wing'd his feet;
As yet Apollo in his radiant seat
Had never driv'n his chariot through the air,
Known by his bow alone and golden hair.
These Jove commission'd to attempt the fray,   180
And rule the sportive military day;
Bid them agree which party each maintains,
And promised a reward that's worth their pains.
The greater took their seats; on either hand
Respectful the less gods in order stand,   185
But careful not to interrupt their play,
By hinting when t' advance or run away.
  Then they examine, who shall first proceed
To try their courage, and their army lead.

Chance gave it for the White, that he should go   190
First with a brave defiance to the foe.
Awhile he ponder'd which of all his train
Should bear his first commission o'er the plain;
And then determined to begin the scene
With him that stood before to guard the Queen.   195
He took a double step: with instant care
Does the black Monarch in his turn prepare
The adverse champion, and with stern command
Bid him repel the charge with equal hand.
There front to front, the midst of all the field,   200
With furious threats their shining arms they wield;
Yet vain the conflict, neither can prevail
While in one path each other they assail.
On ev'ry side to their assistance fly
Their fellow soldiers, and with strong supply   205
Crowd to the battle, but no bloody stain
Tinctures their armour; sportive in the plain
Mars plays awhile, and in excursion slight
Harmless they sally forth, or wait the fight.
 But now the swarthy Foot, that first appear'd   210
To front the foe, his pond'rous jav'lin rear'd
Leftward aslant, and a pale warrior slays,
Spurns him aside, and boldly takes his place.
Unhappy youth, his danger not to spy!
Instant he fell, and triumph'd but to die.   215
At this the sable King with prudent care
Removed his station from the middle square,
And slow retiring to the farthest ground,
There safely lurk'd, with troops entrench'd around.
Then from each quarter to the war advance   220
The furious Knights, and poise the trembling lance:
By turns they rush, by turns the victors yield,
Heaps of dead Foot choke up the crimson'd field:
They fall unable to retreat; around
The clang of arms and iron hoofs resound.   225
 But while young Phoebus pleased himself to view
His furious Knight destroy the vulgar crew,
Sly Hermes long'd t' attempt with secret aim
Some noble act of more exalted fame.
For this, he inoffensive pass'd along   230
Through ranks of Foot, and midst the trembling throng
Sent his left Horse, that free without confine
Rov'd o'er the plain, upon some great design
Against the King himself. At length he stood,
And having fix'd his station as he would,   235
Threaten'd at once with instant fate the King
And th' Indian beast that guarded the right wing.

Apollo sigh'd, and hast'ning to relieve
The straiten'd Monarch, griev'd that he must leave
His martial Elephant expos'd to fate,   240
And view'd with pitying eyes his dang'rous state.
First in his thoughts however was his care
To save his King, whom to the neighbouring square
On the right hand, he snatch'd with trembling flight;
At this with fury springs the sable Knight,   245
Drew his keen sword, and rising to the blow,
Sent the great Indian brute to shades below.
O fatal loss! for none except the Queen
Spreads such a terror through the bloody scene.
Yet shall you ne'er unpunish'd boast your prize,   250
The Delian god with stern resentment cries;
And wedg'd him round with Foot, and pour'd in fresh supplies.
Thus close besieg'd trembling he cast his eye
Around the plain, but saw no shelter nigh,
No way for flight; for here the Queen oppos'd,   255
The Foot in phalanx there the passage clos'd:
At length he fell; yet not unpleas'd with fate,
Since victim to a Queen's vindictive hate.
With grief and fury burns the whiten'd host,
One of their Tow'rs thus immaturely lost.   260
As when a bull has in contention stern
Lost his right horn, with double vengeance burn
His thoughts for war, with blood he's cover'd o'er,
And the woods echo to his dismal roar,
So look'd the flaxen host, when angry fate   265
O'erturn'd the Indian bulwark of their state.
Fired at this great success, with double rage
Apollo hurries on his troops t' engage,
For blood and havoc wild; and, while he leads
His troops thus careless, loses both his steeds: 270
For if some adverse warriors were o'erthrown,
He little thought what dangers threat his own.
But slyer Hermes with observant eyes
March'd slowly cautious, and at distance spies
What moves must next succeed, what dangers next arise.   275
Often would he, the stately Queen to snare,
The slender Foot to front her arms prepare,
And to conceal his scheme he sighs and feigns
Such a wrong step would frustrate all his pains.
Just then an Archer, from the right-hand view,   280
At the pale Queen his arrow boldly drew,
Unseen by Phoebus, who, with studious thought,
From the left side a vulgar hero brought.
But tender Venus, with a pitying eye,
Viewing the sad destruction that was nigh,   285

Wink'd upon Phoebus (for the Goddess sat
By chance directly opposite); at that
Roused in an instant, young Apollo threw
His eyes around the field his troops to view:
Perceiv'd the danger, and with sudden fright   290
Withdrew the Foot that he had sent to fight,
And sav'd his trembling Queen by seasonable flight.
But Maia's son with shouts fill'd all the coast:
The Queen, he cried, the important Queen is lost.
Phoebus, howe'er, resolving to maintain   295
What he had done, bespoke the heavenly train.
What mighty harm, in sportive mimic flight,
Is it to set a little blunder right,
When no preliminary rule debarr'd?
If you henceforward, Mercury, would guard   300
Against such practice, let us make the law:
And whosoe'er shall first to battle draw,
Or white, or black, remorseless let him go
At all events, and dare the angry foe.
  He said, and this opinion pleased around: 305
Jove turn'd aside, and on his daughter frown'd,
Unmark'd by Hermes, who, with strange surprise,
Fretted and foam'd, and roll'd his ferret eyes,
And but with great reluctance could refrain
From dashing at a blow all off the plain.   310
Then he resolved to interweave deceits,—
To carry on the war by tricks and cheats.
Instant he call'd an Archer from the throng,
And bid him like the courser wheel along:
Bounding he springs, and threats the pallid Queen.   315
The fraud, however, was by Phoebus seen;
He smiled, and, turning to the Gods, he said:
Though, Hermes, you are perfect in your trade,
And you can trick and cheat to great surprise,
These little sleights no more shall blind my eyes;   320
Correct them if you please, the more you thus disguise.
The circle laugh'd aloud; and Maia's son
(As if it had but by mistake been done)
Recall'd his Archer, and with motion due,
Bid him advance, the combat to renew.   325
But Phoebus watch'd him with a jealous eye,
Fearing some trick was ever lurking nigh,
For he would oft, with sudden sly design,
Send forth at once two combatants to join
His warring troops, against the law of arms,   330
Unless the wary foe was ever in alarms.
  Now the white Archer with his utmost force
Bent the tough bow against the sable Horse,

And drove him from the Queen, where he had stood
Hoping to glut his vengeance with her blood. 335
Then the right Elephant with martial pride
Roved here and there, and spread his terrors wide:
Glittering in arms from far a courser came,
Threaten'd at once the King and Royal Dame;
Thought himself safe when he the post had seized, 340
And with the future spoils his fancy pleased.
Fired at the danger a young Archer came,
Rush'd on the foe, and levell'd sure his aim;
(And though a Pawn his sword in vengeance draws,
Gladly he'd lose his life in glory's cause). 345
The whistling arrow to his bowels flew,
And the sharp steel his blood profusely drew;
He drops the reins, he totters to the ground,
And his life issued murm'ring through the wound.
Pierced by the Foot, this Archer bit the plain; 350
The Foot himself was by another slain;
And with inflamed revenge, the battle burns again.
Towers, Archers, Knights, meet on the crimson ground,
And the field echoes to the martial sound.
Their thoughts are heated, and their courage fired, 355
Thick they rush on with double zeal inspired;
Generals and Foot, with different colour'd mien,
Confusedly warring in the camps are seen,—
Valour and fortune meet in one promiscuous scene.
Now these victorious, lord it o'er the field; 360
Now the foe rallies, the triumphant yield:
Just as the tide of battle ebbs or flows.
As when the conflict more tempestuous grows
Between the winds, with strong and boisterous sweep
They plough th' Ionian or Atlantic deep! 365
By turns prevail the mutual blustering roar,
And the big waves alternate lash the shore.
  But in the midst of all the battle raged
The snowy Queen, with troops at once engaged;
She fell'd an Archer as she sought the plain,— 370
As she retired an Elephant was slain:
To right and left her fatal spears she sent,
Burst through the ranks, and triumph'd as she went;
Through arms and blood she seeks a glorious fate,
Pierces the farthest lines, and nobly great 375
Leads on her army with a gallant show,
Breaks the battalions, and cuts through the foe.
At length the sable King his fears betray'd,
And begg'd his military consort's aid:
With cheerful speed she flew to his relief, 380
And met in equal arms the female chief.

Who first, great Queen, and who at last did bleed?
How many Whites lay gasping on the mead?
Half dead, and floating in a bloody tide,
Foot, Knights, and Archer lie on every side.   385
Who can recount the slaughter of the day?
How many leaders threw their lives away?
The chequer'd plain is fill'd with dying box,
Havoc ensues, and with tumultuous shocks
The different colour'd ranks in blood engage,   390
And Foot and Horse promiscuously rage.
With nobler courage and superior might
The dreadful Amazons sustain the fight,
Resolved alike to mix in glorious strife,
Till to imperious fate they yield their life.   395
   Meanwhile each Monarch, in a neighbouring cell,
Confined the warriors that in battle fell,
There watch'd the captives with a jealous eye,
Lest, slipping out again, to arms they fly.
But Thracian Mars, in stedfast friendship join'd   400
To Hermes, as near Phoebus he reclined,
Observed each chance, how all their motions bend,
Resolved if possible to serve his friend.
He a Foot-soldier and a Knight purloin'd
Out from the prison that the dead confined;   405
And slyly push'd 'em forward on the plain;
Th' enliven'd combatants their arms regain,
Mix in the bloody scene, and boldly war again.
   So the foul hag, in screaming wild alarms
O'er a dead carcase muttering her charms,   410
(And with her frequent and tremendous yell
Forcing great Hecate from out of hell)
Shoots in the corpse a new fictitious soul;
With instant glare the supple eyeballs roll,
Again it moves and speaks, and life informs the whole. 415
   Vulcan alone discern'd the subtle cheat;
And wisely scorning such a base deceit,
Call'd out to Phoebus. Grief and rage assail
Phoebus by turns; detected Mars turns pale.
Then awful Jove with sullen eye reproved   420
Mars, and the captives order'd to be moved
To their dark caves; bid each fictitious spear
Be straight recall'd, and all be as they were.
   And now both Monarchs with redoubled rage
Led on their Queens, the mutual war to wage.   425
O'er all the field their thirsty spears they send,
Then front to front their Monarchs they defend.
But lo! the female White rush'd in unseen,
And slew with fatal haste the swarthy Queen;

Yet soon, alas! resign'd her royal spoils, 430
Snatch'd by a shaft from her successful toils.
Struck at the sight, both hosts in wild surprise
Pour'd forth their tears, and fill'd the air with cries;
They wept and sigh'd, as pass'd the fun'ral train,
As if both armies had at once been slain. 435
  And now each troop surrounds its mourning chief,
To guard his person, or assuage his grief.
One is their common fear; one stormy blast
Has equally made havoc as it pass'd.
Not all, however, of their youth are slain; 440
Some champions yet the vig'rous war maintain.
Three Foot, an Archer, and a stately Tower,
For Phoebus still exert their utmost power.
Just the same number Mercury can boast,
Except the Tower, who lately in his post 445
Unarm'd inglorious fell, in peace profound,
Pierced by an Archer with a distant wound;
But his right Horse retain'd its mettled pride,—
The rest were swept away by war's strong tide.
  But fretful Hermes, with despairing moan, 450
Griev'd that so many champions were o'erthrown,
Yet reassumes the fight; and summons round
The little straggling army that he found,—
All that had 'scaped from fierce Apollo's rage,—
Resolved with greater caution to engage 455
In future strife, by subtle wiles (if fate
Should give him leave) to save his sinking state.
The sable troops advance with prudence slow,
Bent on all hazards to distress the foe.
More cheerful Phoebus, with unequal pace, 460
Rallies his arms to lessen his disgrace.
But what strange havoc everywhere has been!
A straggling champion here and there is seen;
And many are the tents, yet few are left within.
  Th' afflicted Kings bewail their consorts dead, 465
And loathe the thoughts of a deserted bed;
And though each monarch studies to improve
The tender mem'ry of his former love,
Their state requires a second nuptial tie.
Hence the pale ruler with a love-sick eye 470
Surveys th' attendants of his former wife,
And offers one of them a royal life.
These, when their martial mistress had been slain,
Weak and despairing tried their arms in vain;
Willing, howe'er, amidst the Black to go, 475
They thirst for speedy vengeance on the foe.
Then he resolves to see who merits best,

By strength and courage, the imperial vest;
Points out the foe, bids each with bold design
Pierce through the ranks, and reach the deepest line: 480
For none must hope with monarchs to repose
But who can first, through thick surrounding foes,
Through arms and wiles, with hazardous essay,
Safe to the farthest quarters force their way.
Fired at the thought, with sudden, joyful pace   485
They hurry on; but first of all the race
Runs the third right-hand warrior for the prize,—
The glitt'ring crown already charms her eyes.
Her dear associates cheerfully give o'er
The nuptial chase; and swift she flies before,   490
And Glory lent her wings, and the reward in store.
Nor would the sable King her hopes prevent,
For he himself was on a Queen intent,
Alternate, therefore, through the field they go.
Hermes led on, but by a step too slow,   495
His fourth left Pawn: and now th' advent'rous White
Had march'd through all, and gain'd the wish'd for site.
Then the pleased King gives orders to prepare
The crown, the sceptre, and the royal chair,
And owns her for his Queen: around exult   500
The snowy troops, and o'er the Black insult.
  Hermes burst into tears,—with fretful roar
Fill'd the wide air, and his gay vesture tore.
The swarthy Foot had only to advance
One single step; but oh! malignant chance!   505
A towered Elephant, with fatal aim,
Stood ready to destroy her when she came:
He keeps a watchful eye upon the whole,
Threatens her entrance, and protects the goal.
Meanwhile the royal new-created bride,   510
Pleased with her pomp, spread death and terror wide;
Like lightning through the sable troops she flies,
Clashes her arms, and seems to threat the skies.
The sable troops are sunk in wild affright,
And wish th' earth op'ning snatch'd 'em from her sight.   515
In burst the Queen, with vast impetuous swing:
The trembling foes come swarming round the King,
Where in the midst he stood, and form a valiant ring.
So the poor cows, straggling o'er pasture land,
When they perceive the prowling wolf at hand,   520
Crowd close together in a circle full,
And beg the succour of the lordly bull;
They clash their horns, they low with dreadful sound,
And the remotest groves re-echo round.
  But the bold Queen, victorious, from behind   525

Pierces the foe; yet chiefly she design'd
Against the King himself some fatal aim,
And full of war to his pavilion came.
Now here she rush'd, now there; and had she been
But duly prudent, she had slipp'd between,   530
With course oblique, into the fourth white square,
And the long toil of war had ended there,
The King had fallen, and all his sable state;
And vanquish'd Hermes cursed his partial fate.
For thence with ease the championess might go,   535
Murder the King, and none could ward the blow.
  With silence, Hermes, and with panting heart,
Perceived the danger, but with subtle art,
(Lest he should see the place) spurs on the foe,
Confounds his thoughts, and blames his being slow.   540
For shame! move on; would you for ever stay?
What sloth is this, what strange perverse delay?—
How could you e'er my little pausing blame?—
What! you would wait till night shall end the game?
Phoebus, thus nettled, with imprudence slew   545
A vulgar Pawn, but lost his nobler view.
Young Hermes leap'd, with sudden joy elate;
And then, to save the monarch from his fate,
Led on his martial Knight, who stepp'd between,
Pleased that his charge was to oppose the Queen—   550
Then, pondering how the Indian beast to slay,
That stopp'd the Foot from making farther way,—
From being made a Queen; with slanting aim
An archer struck him; down the monster came,
And dying shook the earth: while Phoebus tries   555
Without success the monarch to surprise.
The Foot, then uncontroll'd with instant pride,
Seized the last spot, and moved a royal bride.
And now with equal strength both war again,
And bring their second wives upon the plain;   560
Then, though with equal views each hop'd and fear'd,
Yet, as if every doubt had disappear'd,
As if he had the palm, young Hermes flies
Into excess of joy; with deep disguise,
Extols his own Black troops, with frequent spite   565
And with invective taunts disdains the White.
Whom Phoebus thus reproved with quick return—
As yet we cannot the decision learn
Of this dispute, and do you triumph now?
Then your big words and vauntings I'll allow,   570
When you the battle shall completely gain;
At present I shall make your boasting vain.
He said, and forward led the daring Queen;

Instant the fury of the bloody scene
Rises tumultuous, swift the warriors fly   575
From either side to conquer or to die.
They front the storm of war: around 'em Fear,
Terror, and Death, perpetually appear.
All meet in arms, and man to man oppose,
Each from their camp attempts to drive their foes;   580
Each tries by turns to force the hostile lines;
Chance and impatience blast their best designs.
The sable Queen spread terror as she went
Through the mid ranks: with more reserved intent
The adverse dame declined the open fray,   585
And to the King in private stole away:
Then took the royal guard, and bursting in,
With fatal menace close besieged the King.
Alarm'd at this, the swarthy Queen, in haste,
From all her havoc and destructive waste   590
Broke off, and her contempt of death to show,
Leap'd in between the Monarch and the foe,
To save the King and state from this impending blow.
But Phoebus met a worse misfortune here:
For Hermes now led forward, void of fear,   595
His furious Horse into the open plain,
That onward chafed, and pranced, and pawed amain.
Nor ceased from his attempts until he stood
On the long-wished-for spot, from whence he could
Slay King or Queen. O'erwhelm'd with sudden fears,   600
Apollo saw, and could not keep from tears.
Now all seem'd ready to be overthrown;
His strength was wither'd, ev'ry hope was flown.
Hermes, exulting at this great surprise,
Shouted for joy, and fill'd the air with cries;   605
Instant he sent the Queen to shades below,
And of her spoils made a triumphant show.
But in return, and in his mid career,
Fell his brave Knight, beneath the Monarch's spear.
  Phoebus, however, did not yet despair,   610
But still fought on with courage and with care.
He had but two poor common men to show,
And Mars's favourite with his iv'ry bow.
The thoughts of ruin made 'em dare their best
To save their King, so fatally distress'd.   615
But the sad hour required not such an aid;
And Hermes breathed revenge where'er he stray'd.
Fierce comes the sable Queen with fatal threat,
Surrounds the Monarch in his royal seat;
Rushed here and there, nor rested till she slew   620
The last remainder of the whiten'd crew.

Sole stood the King, the midst of all the plain,
Weak and defenceless, his companions slain.
As when the ruddy morn ascending high
Has chased the twinkling stars from all the sky,   625
Your star, fair Venus, still retains its light,
And, loveliest, goes the latest out of sight.
No safety's left, no gleams of hope remain;
Yet did he not as vanquish'd quit the plain,
But tried to shut himself between the foe,—   630
Unhurt through swords and spears he hoped to go,
Until no room was left to shun the fatal blow.
For if none threaten'd his immediate fate,
And his next move must ruin all his state,
All their past toil and labour is in vain,   635
Vain all the bloody carnage of the plain,—
Neither would triumph then, the laurel neither gain.
Therefore through each void space and desert tent,
By different moves his various course he bent:
The Black King watch'd him with observant eye,   640
Follow'd him close, but left him room to fly.
Then when he saw him take the farthest line,
He sent the Queen his motions to confine,
And guard the second rank, that he could go
No farther now than to that distant row.   645
The sable monarch then with cheerful mien
Approach'd, but always with one space between.
But as the King stood o'er against him there,
Helpless, forlorn, and sunk in his despair,
The martial Queen her lucky moment knew,   650
Seized on the farthest seat with fatal view,
Nor left th' unhappy King a place to flee unto.
At length in vengeance her keen sword she draws,
Slew him, and ended thus the bloody cause:
And all the gods around approved it with applause.   655
  The victor could not from his insults keep,
But laugh'd and sneer'd to see Apollo weep.
Jove call'd him near, and gave him in his hand
The powerful, happy, and mysterious wand
By which the Shades are call'd to purer day,   660
When penal fire has purged their sins away;
By which the guilty are condemn'd to dwell
In the dark mansions of the deepest hell;
By which he gives us sleep, or sleep denies,
And closes at the last the dying eyes.   665
Soon after this, the heavenly victor brought
The game on earth, and first th' Italians taught.
  For (as they say) fair Scacchis he espied
Feeding her cygnets in the silver tide,

(Sacchis, the loveliest Seriad of the place) 670
And as she stray'd, took her to his embrace.
Then, to reward her for her virtue lost,
Gave her the men and chequer'd board, emboss'd
With gold and silver curiously inlay'd;
And taught her how the game was to be play'd. 675
Ev'n now 'tis honour'd with her happy name;
And Rome and all the world admire the game.
All which the Seriads told me heretofore,
When my boy-notes amused the Serian shore.

NOTES

i   This is the usual account. But it was maintained by the family of the poet's mother, and has been contended (by Dr. Michael F. Cox in a Lecture on 'The Country and Kindred of Oliver Goldsmith,' published in vol. 1, pt. 2, of the *Journal* of the 'National Literary Society of Ireland.' 1900) that his real birth-place was the residence of Mrs. Goldsmith's parents, Smith-Hill House, Elphin, Roscommon, to which she was in the habit of paying frequent visits. Meanwhile, in 1897, a window was placed to Goldsmith's memory in Forgney Church, Longford,—the church of which, at the time of his birth, his father was curate.

ii   'Oliver Goldsmith is recorded on two occasions as being remarkably diligent at Morning Lecture; again, as cautioned for bad answering at Morning and Greek Lectures; and finally, as put down into the next class for neglect of his studies' (Dr. Stubbs's *History of the University of Dublin*, 1889, p. 201 n.)

iii   This, which is now at Trinity College, Dublin, is here reproduced in facsimile. When the garrets of No. 35, Parliament Square, were pulled down in 1837, it was cut out of the window by the last occupant of the rooms, who broke it in the process. (Dr. J. F. Waller in Cassell's *Works* of Goldsmith, [1864–5], pp. xiii–xiv n.)

iv   Where he obtained his diploma is not known. It was certainly not at Padua (*Athenaeum*, July 21, 1894). At Leyden and Louvain Prior made inquiries but, in each case, without success. The annals of the University of Louvain were, however, destroyed in the revolutionary wars. (Prior, *Life*, 1837, i, pp. 171, 178).

v   Goldsmith's authorship of this version has now been placed beyond a doubt by the publication in facsimile of his signed receipt to Edward Dilly for third share of 'my translation,' such third share amounting to 6 pounds 13s. 4d. The receipt, which belongs to Mr. J. W. Ford of Enfield Old Park, is dated 'January 11th, 1758.' (*Memoirs of a Protestant*, etc., Dent's edition, 1895, i, pp. xii–xviii.)

vi   This was a tiny square occupying a site now absorbed by the Holborn Viaduct and Railway Station. No. 12, where Goldsmith lived, was later occupied by Messrs. Smith, Elder & Co. as a printing office. An engraving of the Court forms the frontispiece to the *European Magazine* for January, 1803.

vii   The proximate cause of the *Citizen of the World*, as the present writer has suggested elsewhere, *may* have been Horace Walpole's *Letter from XoHo* [Soho?], *a Chinese Philosopher at London, to his friend Lien Chi, at Peking*. This was noticed as 'in Montesquieu's manner' in the May issue of the *Monthly Review* for 1757, to which Goldsmith was a contributor (*Eighteenth Century Vignettes*, first series, second edition, 1897, pp. 108–9).

viii   e.g.—The references to the musical glasses (ch. ix), which were the rage in 1761–2; and to the *Auditor* (ch. xix) established by Arthur Murphy in June of the latter year. The sale of the 'Vicar' is discussed at length in chapter vii of the editor's *Life of Oliver Goldsmith* ('Great Writers' series), 1888, pp. 110–21.

ix   This, which to some critics has seemed unintelligible, rests upon the following: 'The first three editions, . . . resulted in a loss, and the fourth, which was not issued until eight [four?] years after the first, started with a balance against it of £2 16s. 6d., and it was not until that fourth edition had been sold that the balance came out on the right side' (*A Bookseller of the Last Century* [John

Newbery] by Charles Welsh, 1885, p. 61). The writer based his statement upon Collins's 'Publishing book, account of books printed and shares therein, No. 3, 1770 to 1785.'

x   This was a famous patent panacea, invented by Johnson's Lichfield townsman, Dr. Robert James of the *Medicinal Dictionary*. It was sold by John Newbery, and had an extraordinary vogue. The King dosed Princess Elizabeth with it; Fielding, Gray, and Cowper all swore by it, and Horace Walpole, who wished to try it upon Mme. du Deffand *in extremis*, said he should use it if the house were on fire. William Hawes, the Strand apothecary who attended Goldsmith, wrote an interesting *Account of the late Dr. Goldsmith's Illness, so far as relates to the Exhibition of Dr. James's Powders,* etc., 1774, which he dedicated to Reynolds and Burke. To Hawes once belonged the poet's worn old wooden writing-desk, now in the South Kensington Museum, where are also his favourite chair and cane. Another desk-chair, which had descended from his friend, Edmund Bott, was recently for sale at Sotheby's (July, 1906).